Arcturian Energy
Exploring the Fifth Dimension
Luiz Santos

Copyright © 2022 Luiz Santos
All rights reserved.
No part of this book may be reproduced in any form or by any means without written permission from the copyright holder.
Cover image © Vellaz Studio
Review by Armando Vellaz
Graphic design by Amadeu Brumm
Layout by Matheus Costa
All rights reserved to:
Luiz A. Santos
Category: Holism

Summary

Prologue 4
Chapter 1 Arcturian Connection 8
Chapter 2 Spiritual Preparation 15
Chapter 3 Energy Alignment 20
Chapter 4 Arcturian Channeling 26
Chapter 5 Self-Healing 32
Chapter 6 Healing for Others 38
Chapter 7 Expansion of Consciousness 44
Chapter 8 Higher Dimensions 50
Chapter 9 Personal Transformation 56
Chapter 10 Arcturian Meditations 62
Chapter 11 Advanced Energy Healing 68
Chapter 12 Energy Protection 74
Chapter 13 Healing Crystals 80
Chapter 14 Collective Rituals 86
Chapter 15 Daily Integration 92
Chapter 16 Spiritual Awakening 99
Chapter 17 Arcturian Intuition 106
Chapter 18 Group Practices 113
Chapter 19 Deep Meditation 120
Chapter 20 Advanced Channeling 126
Chapter 21 Earth Healing 133
Chapter 22 Daily Practice 139
Chapter 23 Spiritual Integration 145
Chapter 24 Collective Journey 150

Chapter 25 Social Projects 156
Chapter 26 Collective Elevation 162
Chapter 27 Planetary Consciousness 168
Chapter 28 Collective Transcendence... 174
Epilogue 180

Prologue

The book you hold in your hands is more than just words; it is a portal. By opening it, you are embarking on a journey that transcends time and space, touching the hidden layers of your being. This is no ordinary invitation. It is a vibrant call, brimming with a wisdom that pulses between the lines, in the nuances of each word, like a whisper from the stars. Here, you will not find theories or superficial concepts; this book is a map drawn for those who seek to awaken their consciousness—a journey that reaches beyond what we know as reality. The Arcturians, beings of pure light and wisdom, guide you toward dimensions of existence where time and space dissolve, where your own essence resonates with the heartbeat of the cosmos.

As you read these pages, you'll sense that every line was placed here to speak directly to your soul, as though the author had listened to the secrets of the universe and translated them so you could understand. There is no coincidence in your choice to read this book. Something within you is ready to receive the energy it transmits, to access frequencies of light that reveal the invisible, that awaken your own hidden power. This is a meeting between your awareness and universal truth, mediated by teachings that transcend cultural boundaries and human limitations.

As you continue reading, doors to new perceptions will open before you. You will see that reality is not what it seems; that you are far more than the sum of your thoughts, your memories, and your experiences. You will feel the connection to the All That Is, that which surrounds and guides you, even if unseen. The Arcturians offer us a silent invitation to deep transformation, but it is up to you to accept this call, to open yourself to their energy, and to allow it to penetrate the deepest corners of your soul. They are here to help you awaken, to lift the veil that covers your true purpose, and to guide you back to the path of harmony and healing.

As you follow the path within these pages, you will know you are on a journey of no return, where every word, every idea, every practice offered is a step closer to self-discovery, preparing you to attune to higher dimensions. This book is like a compass, pointing toward a new reality where healing, love, and wisdom are your guides. You will be led to discover that you are not alone; that enlightened beings accompany you and offer the tools necessary to transform your existence, to elevate your consciousness, and to awaken the dormant abilities within you.

This is not merely a reading; it is an experience, a journey that calls you to respond with your own energy. The words here carry a unique vibration, like an ancient code that only the prepared can access. It is an invitation to dive into your own essence, to allow your frequency to align with higher vibrations, harmonizing with the pulse of the universe. This is no ordinary reading; it is a gateway to experiences, a journey that enables you to resonate with Arcturian wisdom, a wisdom that transcends thought and speaks directly to the heart.

Prepare yourself, for this book was written for you. It will unfold possibilities in your life that you may never have imagined. As you advance, you will realize that the practices and teachings resonate within you, awakening ancient memories, activating parts of your being that were once dormant. Here, you will find tools to cultivate inner peace, expand your perception, and, above all, recognize the interconnectedness of all that exists. This is a path of ascension, where self-knowledge transforms into a state of being, where your essence rises and shines.

So allow yourself. Let the energy of this book surround you, let its wisdom reveal itself on each page, transforming your understanding of existence, of your role in the universe. Remember, each revelation here is a call to awaken, to claim your place in this vastness of light and consciousness. This is the beginning of a journey that will lead you to your deepest truth, to your connection with the mysteries of the cosmos, with the essence of life. Feel each word as a key, open your mind and heart to what you are about to experience. After all, this book was written for you.

Chapter 1
Arcturian Connection

In the quiet folds of the cosmos, beyond the far reaches of known stars, there resides a consciousness woven of light, knowledge, and a love as vast as the sky. The Arcturians—celestial guides whose origins trace back to eons beyond human memory—exist as silent, compassionate caretakers of spiritual evolution. Their presence is like a beacon in the universe, reaching out to touch and guide those ready to transcend the confines of earthly understanding. Humanity's connection to these beings holds a profound purpose: to remember the ancient spiritual mission lying dormant within, to heal, and to awaken to a shared journey of self-discovery and collective ascension.

It is said that the Arcturians carry an awareness of energy and consciousness that is light-years beyond earthly understanding, vibrating at frequencies so fine that only the most open hearts sense their touch. To understand the Arcturians is to begin a journey into a place where time dissolves, where energy flows like rivers of light, and where the mind quiets as the spirit awakens to its own boundless nature. Who they are may forever remain a mystery, but their mission is clear: to lift humanity from darkness, guiding it toward inner transformation, harmony, and connection with the cosmic currents of love and wisdom.

In the moments when the veil between worlds thins, some feel a gentle, almost imperceptible presence, as if surrounded by a comforting force that seems to know them intimately. This is the subtle signature of the Arcturian connection. Their purpose is not to impose or interfere; it is to inspire, to extend their presence as guides, offering the soft strength of their energy as a mirror to awaken us to our own potential. This connection vibrates with a quiet but enduring frequency, touching each person with a unique resonance, as if speaking directly to their innermost self. Those who feel called toward this connection do so not out of chance but as a response to an invitation woven through lifetimes and dimensions.

The journey of Arcturian connection becomes a path of self-rediscovery, but it is one that extends beyond the individual. Each step, each moment of awakening, unfolds as part of a greater mission—a mission that reverberates throughout humanity and reaches into the heart of Earth itself. As this connection takes root, practitioners often find themselves aligned with a profound purpose, realizing that each personal healing, each insight gained, echoes into the fabric of humanity's collective consciousness. The Arcturians inspire this awareness, teaching us that our existence is interwoven with the lives of others, with the planet, and with realms unseen.

Experiences with the Arcturians can manifest in ways that defy logical explanation, often appearing as symbols in dreams, flashes of insight during meditation, or an inexplicable feeling of peace during times of hardship. For many, these encounters become a sacred reminder of a spiritual lineage reaching back to the stars, as if the Arcturians have always been present, quietly observing, waiting for us to seek the light that they so gently offer. Their presence opens the doors of intuition and insight, helping individuals understand life beyond the limits of the visible and the known.

And so, with this deepening of connection, we come to an understanding that the journey is as much an inward exploration as it is a shared, cosmic undertaking. Through their guidance, the Arcturians awaken humanity to the realization that each step toward personal healing and growth contributes to the ascension of the whole, rippling outward like waves of light. We begin to feel that our connection with them is not for personal empowerment alone but is a gift that can help bring humanity into an era of shared understanding and elevated consciousness.

In surrendering to this connection, one steps into an energy that is both comforting and transformative. The Arcturians are said to inspire practices that help one go beyond ego, to lay down old patterns of thought and belief, and to step into the clarity of being. It is a process that guides practitioners to cultivate virtues of compassion, patience, and inner peace. These virtues are not mere ideals but keys that unlock the doors of higher awareness, gradually leading each soul closer to the resonance of the Arcturians and, ultimately, to the light within themselves.

As Earth continues its journey through an age of transformation, the Arcturians extend their energy to those ready to serve as conduits of healing, compassion, and clarity. They remind us that the true purpose of awakening lies not in personal enlightenment alone but in uplifting others and in restoring harmony to the planet. Through this bond, we sense an ancient alignment, a subtle but powerful impulse to join hands in collective growth. The Arcturians call each person to become not only seekers of light but also carriers of light, illuminating the path for others and becoming agents of a new, conscious era.

Arcturian contact, then, is not so much a destination as it is an unfolding journey. It brings into being a deeper understanding of oneself, touching aspects of spirit that lie beyond language and concept. Through connection with the Arcturians, we remember that our place in the universe is one of interdependence, that the evolution of each soul contributes to the greater ascension of all beings. This relationship offers wisdom that empowers us to live with a new depth of awareness, nurturing qualities of compassion and peace that elevate every interaction, every thought, and every choice.

For those stepping onto this path, the Arcturian presence is a gentle guide, a profound teacher, and a reminder of our own luminous essence. It is an invitation to shed the illusions of separation and limitation, to embrace the journey of healing and to reawaken to the truth that we are, each of us, deeply connected to a loving universe. As one attunes to their frequency, an invisible hand seems to guide the soul through both the quiet and the storms of life, holding a light that never wavers and encouraging each step toward wholeness.

In the stillness of connection, we come to recognize that the Arcturians are not distant beings but kindred souls, reflections of the divine potential within us all. They lead us not toward themselves but toward the depths of our own hearts, showing that the journey is both ancient and new, as boundless as the cosmos itself and as close as our own breath. Through this bond, we learn that each moment of growth, each choice for love and compassion, brings us closer to the radiant truth of our shared existence, bridging dimensions and worlds in the endless dance of light.

In the silence that follows the first touch of Arcturian energy, a deeper current begins to flow. Those who seek to strengthen this connection find themselves called to go beyond the abstract, to experience the Arcturian resonance as a living presence within and around them. The journey is intimate, quiet, a soft immersion into energies that transcend understanding but which the heart seems to recognize. To anchor this connection, one must step into a meditative stillness, into practices that open a doorway within, allowing the practitioner's energy to gradually align with the higher frequency of the Arcturians.

Meditation forms the foundation of this alignment. Through disciplined practice, the mind quiets, allowing the practitioner to feel a shift in awareness as subtle energies move from deep within, meeting those from beyond. By sitting in the gentle stillness of meditation, one begins to attune to the finer vibrations that characterize Arcturian presence. This practice is not about silence for silence's sake but about opening an inner space where a distinct awareness, pure and undistracted, can emerge. And as one deepens into this meditative field, a sense of familiarity often arises—a feeling of being surrounded by an invisible presence that is as real and tangible as the breath itself.

Visualization becomes a bridge in these practices, guiding the practitioner into a space where the senses expand beyond the physical. Imagining oneself bathed in blue or violet light, the colors associated with Arcturian energy, one begins to feel a soothing, magnetic pull toward a state of balance and clarity. These colors are often perceived as carriers of wisdom and healing, each shade resonating with a quality of peace and higher knowledge. By allowing this light to envelop the mind and heart, one senses an uplifting of vibration, a soft opening to a deeper experience of connection.

In these moments of visualization, practitioners may notice a clarity within themselves that feels as though they have awakened to an inner voice, one that gently guides them, resonating with an ancient familiarity. This voice is not so much spoken as it is felt—a clear and grounded intuition that brings messages of healing, encouragement, and clarity. And while it may feel subtle at first, like a barely perceptible whisper, over time, practitioners find this intuition strengthening, becoming a true channel for guidance that feels both wise and compassionate.

Another tool on this path is breathwork. Conscious breathing allows the practitioner to bring focus inward, to calm the restless waves of thought and emotion, preparing the inner self to fully receive the connection. Deep, intentional breathing acts as a reminder of the simplicity and beauty of each moment. By cultivating a breath pattern that is slow and measured, practitioners create a rhythm that harmonizes with the steady, serene energy of the Arcturians. As one breathes, an internal shift happens, a subtle alignment that brings the Arcturian frequency closer, as if they are there, right within reach. Breath becomes a bridge that transports one from the realm of the seen into the uncharted domains of spirit.

Trust in the connection is essential. As practitioners deepen these exercises, they begin to feel an increasing openness, a sensitivity to energies that may at first seem unfamiliar but which over time bring a profound sense of peace and trust. Each meditation, each visualization, builds upon the last, and soon, an inner certainty emerges—an assurance that the connection is real, that it is one that has been patiently awaiting this recognition. The more one surrenders to this trust, the more vivid and enriched the experience becomes, creating a spiritual bond that feels grounded, nourishing, and protective.

As this bond strengthens, signs may appear in unexpected ways, confirming the presence of the Arcturians. Practitioners often experience synchronicities, dreams, or subtle hints from the universe—a number repeated in unexpected places, an image, or a word that calls attention. These moments serve as reminders, gentle affirmations of the Arcturian presence, echoing through the fabric of daily life. They bring the connection from the depths of meditation into the ordinary, weaving a thread of divine guidance into the mundane.

For those who feel called to deepen this connection, establishing a daily practice is invaluable. Setting aside time, even if brief, for meditation, visualization, and breathing helps sustain and enrich the connection. Creating a sacred space for practice—a simple arrangement with candles, crystals, or items that hold personal significance—can help foster an environment of peace and readiness. This place becomes a sanctuary, a silent temple in which the Arcturian frequency can be felt more tangibly, providing a container for growth, discovery, and healing.

Through these practices, practitioners cultivate a refined awareness, an openness that resonates with the frequency of the Arcturians. The journey becomes one of unfolding rather than striving, a process that happens as naturally as a flower blooming. Trust deepens, and the connection grows into a bond that is felt not only during meditation but in each interaction, each thought, as a subtle influence guiding the practitioner's actions with compassion, clarity, and an increasing sense of purpose.

As practitioners grow in their connection, many find themselves feeling more grounded, at peace with their purpose, and more connected to the web of life. This alignment with the Arcturians fosters qualities of resilience, intuition, and an inner calm that empowers practitioners to navigate the complexities of life with a steady heart. They become not only connected to the

Arcturians but also more attuned to their own essence, to the truth that lives within, guiding them with wisdom and love.

Chapter 2
Spiritual Preparation

The first whispers of a genuine Arcturian connection demand more than desire; they require a clear, intentional spirit prepared to embrace the subtleties of a higher frequency. To stand in the fullness of this energy, one must cultivate an inner environment of readiness, free of the debris of daily anxieties and chaotic energies. This preparation, like the steady chime of a bell, calls practitioners to clean and align their energy bodies, shaping themselves into receptive vessels for Arcturian wisdom and guidance.

Energy cleansing is the first essential practice on this path. By cleansing one's energy field, practitioners shed the layers of residue that accumulate through daily interactions, emotions, and stresses. These invisible layers, though intangible, can dull one's sensitivity to higher vibrations and obscure the clarity required for connection. With each cleansing, the energy body becomes lighter, as if lifting a veil between one's everyday awareness and the profound presence of higher realms.

One of the most effective methods for this cleansing is through grounding. To ground oneself is to connect energetically with Earth's stabilizing energy, drawing upon its steadying force to clear and recharge. Through visualization, practitioners imagine their energy extending like roots deep into the soil, absorbing Earth's nurturing, purifying qualities. As they breathe, they release any stagnant energy down into the ground, where it is transmuted and neutralized. This grounding practice becomes a foundational ritual, providing stability and creating a sanctuary of inner calm from which the Arcturian connection can grow.

Alongside grounding, energy alignment becomes another pillar of spiritual preparation. Alignment practices focus on harmonizing the energy centers, or chakras, allowing them to flow smoothly and freely. Each chakra functions as a conduit for different aspects of consciousness, and when these energy centers are aligned, they create a pathway that elevates the practitioner's vibration. The process begins at the base, grounding one's energy, and then moves upward, activating the centers for creativity, power, compassion, and vision, until reaching the crown, the portal to the spiritual realms. This alignment of the chakras creates a harmonious internal environment that resonates with Arcturian energy, allowing their presence to be felt with greater ease and clarity.

Intention setting is another key practice in preparing for this connection. Each person's intention serves as a beacon, a distinct frequency that calls forth energies aligned with their purpose and desire. By setting a sincere, clear intention to connect with the Arcturians, practitioners send a message across the subtle realms, an invitation that says, "I am ready." This intention creates a vibrational signature, an energy pattern that begins to attract the guidance and support needed for the journey. The Arcturians respond not to words but to the heart's resonance, to the purity of one's purpose. When practitioners set their intentions with honesty and openness, they create an energetic bridge, a pathway for connection that is as real as any physical road.

Visualizations and mantras can deepen this intention. Visualizing an energy sphere surrounding oneself, filled with light, can enhance the feeling of protection and clarity. This sphere acts as both a shield and a filter, keeping one's energy aligned and amplifying the connection. Reciting mantras or affirmations also helps stabilize intention, grounding it in the physical world. Phrases like "I open myself to the guidance of the Arcturians" or "May I be a clear channel for light and wisdom" carry a resonance that permeates through one's energy, filling every cell and thought with purpose. Through these practices, practitioners fortify their inner space, creating a sanctuary where Arcturian energy can be received.

This preparation goes beyond individual practices; it becomes a lifestyle of subtle shifts in awareness and action. The food one eats, the thoughts one entertains, the places one visits—all leave an imprint on the energy body. By cultivating mindfulness in daily life, practitioners begin to notice how each choice and action affects their energetic balance. Every intentional act, every mindful moment, becomes part of the foundation for connection, raising the frequency with which they meet the world and deepening their alignment with higher energies. This awareness ripples through each layer of being, grounding them in a purity of purpose.

With every cleansing, every intention, and every mindful choice, practitioners build a resonance that prepares them not only for connection with the Arcturians but for their own transformation. As they clear the inner pathways, they open to the flow of energy and wisdom that surrounds them, moving in harmony with a rhythm that has existed since the dawn of time.

Beyond the initial steps of spiritual cleansing and intention setting, the journey deepens. Preparation for the Arcturian connection involves not only aligning one's own energy but also building a stable, protective environment around this energy. As practitioners refine their practices, they learn to create a field of light and protection, a space that preserves the purity of the connection and safeguards the journey. This step is essential, as it offers both a sanctuary and a compass, ensuring that every encounter with the Arcturian frequency is anchored in clarity and light.

The creation of a protective environment begins with the practice of sacred space. This space can be a physical location—an altar, a meditation room, or simply a dedicated corner in the home—but its essence is energetic. Through visualization, practitioners create a space filled with light, imbued with intention, where they feel at peace and connected. This area, however small, becomes a point of resonance, a space where higher energies naturally gather. Practitioners often visualize the area surrounded by a golden or violet light, allowing this light to act as a shield, gently deterring any energies that may disrupt the connection.

Sacred sound plays a transformative role here, often invoked through chanting, music, or the quiet repetition of mantras. These sounds are not merely pleasing to the ear; they vibrate with frequencies that purify the energy field, raising the vibration within the environment. Practitioners may choose a mantra, a sacred word or phrase that resonates with their intention, and repeat it, allowing the sound to dissolve any lingering energetic impurities. As this sound reverberates, it fills the space, creating a vibration that is harmonious, protective, and inviting to higher energies.

Visualizations also serve as powerful tools in this phase of preparation. A common practice is to envision a column of light descending from above, enveloping the practitioner and extending into the earth below. This light acts as a protective shield, fortifying the aura and connecting it to both the heavens and the earth. Some practitioners add another layer, visualizing a sphere of light around their body that reflects only the purest energies, filtering out any vibrations that do not resonate with their highest intentions. This imagery is not merely mental but works on an energetic level, helping to create an aura that is aligned, secure, and open to the Arcturian frequency.

As preparation continues, the use of specific mantras deepens the experience, enhancing both protection and connection. Sacred phrases, whether in one's native language or in the form of ancient Arcturian sounds, are thought to carry vibrations that resonate with higher realms. By repeating a chosen mantra or affirmation, practitioners stabilize their energy, forming a bridge that aligns them with Arcturian presence. The vibration of these mantras reaches into the deepest layers of consciousness, where they resonate as more than sound; they become an invitation to the Arcturians, a clear signal that the practitioner's energy is open and ready.

The atmosphere created through these practices not only prepares practitioners but also attracts energies that are in harmony with their intentions. As their energy field stabilizes, practitioners may begin to sense a new clarity, a heightened sensitivity to subtle shifts around them. They become attuned to the flow of energy, recognizing the protective embrace of their environment and feeling a renewed confidence in their connection. The space they have created becomes an energetic foundation, a home for their spirit, where the light of the Arcturians is received and amplified.

These preparatory steps culminate in an energy that is resilient, a refined frequency that resonates with strength and compassion. Practitioners find that, within this protected space, they are more receptive, able to experience the Arcturian presence with clarity and without interference. With every repetition of a mantra, every visualization of light, the connection deepens, laying the groundwork for the next stages of healing, exploration, and the profound journey toward spiritual alignment.

Chapter 3
Energy Alignment

Energy alignment is the silent dance of the inner world, a path to coherence that touches each layer of the self. This alignment is not merely a preparation; it is a state of being where all levels of consciousness—mind, body, and spirit—merge in harmony. For practitioners seeking an authentic connection with the Arcturian presence, understanding and balancing the energy centers, or chakras, becomes essential. Each chakra is like a gateway, a vital part of the energetic landscape that, when balanced, invites clarity, healing, and resonance with higher frequencies.

At the base of this journey lies the Root Chakra, the center of stability and grounding, where the practitioner's connection to Earth finds its strength. When in balance, this chakra provides a sense of security, anchoring the individual firmly in the present and creating a foundation from which higher energies can be accessed. Practitioners visualize this energy center as a red, glowing light that pulses with life, grounding them into the earth. This grounding connects not only to the physical but also to an ancient, unspoken wisdom that lies deep within, establishing a foundation of resilience and safety.

Rising from this foundation, the energy flows upward to the Sacral Chakra, the center of creativity and emotional resonance. This chakra is represented by a warm orange light and governs the flow of emotions, the seat of one's creative power and intuitive knowing. For the Arcturian connection to flourish, this energy center must be in balance, allowing emotions to move freely without stagnation. By gently opening this chakra, practitioners foster a connection that is both fluid and adaptive, a readiness to embrace the unknown with trust and open-heartedness.

The next gateway, the Solar Plexus Chakra, shines with a brilliant yellow light, embodying the essence of willpower and personal strength. Here, energy coalesces as self-confidence and inner purpose, qualities that are essential for those on a path of spiritual discovery. A balanced Solar Plexus enables practitioners to stand firm in their truth, guided by an inner knowing that remains steady even amidst uncertainty. Visualizing this chakra as a radiant sun within, practitioners harness its energy, strengthening their will and aligning their intentions with a purpose greater than themselves.

Further up, the Heart Chakra, glowing with a soft green or pink light, is the center of unconditional love and compassion. Here lies the bridge between the lower and higher energies, a space where empathy and unity reside. For those connecting with the Arcturians, an open and balanced Heart Chakra is essential, as it allows them to experience the subtle frequencies of love and support emanating from these beings. Through this heart-centered connection, practitioners come to feel the gentle, compassionate presence of the Arcturians, as if held in a space of deep acceptance. This is where separation dissolves, and the heart becomes the true compass, guiding them toward healing and connection.

Moving into the realms of communication and insight, the Throat Chakra glows with a clear blue light, the center of expression and truth. Here, practitioners cultivate the ability to communicate their intentions with clarity and honesty. This chakra becomes particularly relevant when receiving or sharing messages from the Arcturians, as it supports the alignment between inner truths and outer expressions. Through visualization, practitioners open this energy center, allowing their voice to resonate with authenticity and connecting their insights with words that convey their essence.

Ascending to the Third Eye Chakra, a deep indigo light opens the pathway of intuition and vision. This is the center of inner sight, where one's perception expands beyond the physical and touches the realms of spirit. In aligning with the Arcturians, the Third Eye serves as a lens for perceiving messages, symbols, and energies from beyond the veil. Through focused meditation on this chakra, practitioners cultivate a sensitivity to the subtle impressions that carry the essence of Arcturian wisdom. This vision is not confined to sight; it is a knowing, a sense that comes from deep within and extends outward, guiding practitioners to trust their intuition.

At the top of the energetic field, the Crown Chakra glows with a violet or white light, the doorway to the divine and to the unity of all things. This chakra transcends the individual, connecting them with the universal consciousness, the oneness that the Arcturians embody. A balanced Crown Chakra aligns practitioners with higher states of awareness, creating an open channel for Arcturian energy to flow freely. Through this alignment, they experience a profound unity, sensing the interconnectedness of all beings and touching the infinite potential of the cosmos.

Together, these seven centers create a pathway that allows the practitioner to move into alignment, each chakra acting as a tuning fork, resonating with the higher frequencies of the Arcturian connection. In this balanced state, energy flows naturally, without blockages, inviting the presence of the Arcturians with ease and clarity. This alignment becomes more than a practice; it is a living experience, a state of harmony that brings light to the mind and peace to the heart, preparing the practitioner for a deeper journey into healing, insight, and spiritual growth.

As the journey into energy alignment unfolds, each chakra becomes not only a center of personal power but a bridge to higher realms. Practitioners seeking a deeper Arcturian connection discover that through specific alignment techniques, they can amplify the flow of energy, enhancing both inner balance and the resonance necessary to receive Arcturian guidance. This alignment creates a vessel ready to hold and transmit healing energy, allowing the practitioner to serve as a clear channel for transformation. The journey through alignment now expands with practices designed to refine, activate, and integrate these energy centers with precision and intention.

Crystals serve as essential allies in this phase, offering vibrational support to each chakra. Each crystal, chosen carefully for its resonance, holds a frequency that can stimulate, balance, or calm specific energy centers, enhancing the alignment process. For the Root Chakra, a grounding stone such as hematite or red jasper is ideal, anchoring the practitioner in Earth's stabilizing energy. For the Sacral Chakra, carnelian or moonstone is often used, promoting emotional flow and creative energy. As practitioners work with each stone, they place it near or upon the corresponding chakra, closing their eyes and breathing with the crystal's vibration, sensing how it amplifies the energy within and around them. These stones act as silent guides, resonating in harmony with the Arcturian frequency and bringing clarity to each center.

One powerful practice involves placing crystals in a line along the chakras during meditation, creating a channel that harmonizes the entire energy body. In this practice, practitioners feel each stone's frequency, imagining the energy flowing upward in a continuous line, connecting each center from the Root to the Crown. As they breathe, they visualize this energy as a steady river of light, cleansing and aligning. The Arcturians often communicate through subtle impressions, and this crystalline alignment allows the energy to remain open and receptive, creating a channel that welcomes their presence with grace and balance.

Arcturian light techniques also provide invaluable support in energy alignment. By visualizing specific colors associated with each chakra, practitioners activate and balance the centers through light and intention. For example, envisioning a brilliant red light at the Root Chakra or a serene green light at the Heart

Chakra can cleanse and invigorate these areas. These visualizations are more than imaginative exercises; they resonate with the Arcturian light, a frequency said to carry a purity that transcends earthly densities. By focusing on these colors, practitioners align each chakra to a higher vibration, creating an atmosphere of healing and openness.

In addition to crystal work and light techniques, sound frequencies play a transformative role. Tuning forks or singing bowls, tuned to the frequency of each chakra, create sound waves that penetrate deep into the energy centers, releasing tension and clearing stagnation. The sound resonates within the body, creating a harmonious frequency that allows each chakra to vibrate with clarity and precision. When the Arcturian frequency blends with this sound, the experience often deepens, as if a door to a higher awareness opens, allowing practitioners to feel not only their own energy but the presence of other realms.

The breath itself becomes an alignment tool, acting as a gentle guide that leads energy upward through each center. Practitioners practice breathing exercises, directing their breath to each chakra, one by one, as if filling each with light and space. By inhaling deeply and exhaling slowly, they visualize each chakra expanding, allowing more light, more energy, and more clarity. This breathwork integrates the different techniques—crystal, light, and sound—into a unified practice, creating a seamless flow of energy that connects the physical, emotional, and spiritual layers of the self.

In the stillness that follows these practices, practitioners often experience a heightened sense of presence, an inner calm that signifies true alignment. This state of alignment becomes more than preparation; it is the foundation from which the Arcturian connection blossoms. With each technique, each intentional breath, they prepare their energy body to serve as a conduit for Arcturian healing, creating a path that leads to the heart of spiritual exploration, connection, and unity. The harmony established within becomes a mirror, reflecting the harmony of the universe and opening the door to realms of higher consciousness and healing.

Chapter 4
Arcturian Channeling

The practice of channeling is a journey into subtle realms, where the boundaries of self and spirit dissolve, and messages from higher beings can reach the depths of the mind and heart. For those drawn to connect with the Arcturians, channeling becomes a profound gateway. It allows practitioners to tap into an ancient wisdom, receiving guidance and insight from those whose purpose is to aid humanity's evolution. Yet channeling is not a casual endeavor; it is a discipline that calls for both openness and careful preparation, for it is only in a refined state of mental clarity and spiritual intention that the Arcturian energy can truly enter and flow.

Channeling begins by cultivating a receptive state of mind. Meditation plays an essential role here, creating a quiet mental space where the natural chatter of thoughts subsides. Practitioners close their eyes, breathe slowly, and allow their minds to rest, clearing away distractions. With each breath, they imagine a vast, open space forming within—a place that feels peaceful, boundless, and safe. In this quiet, they invite the presence of the Arcturians, opening themselves to receive their wisdom with humility and respect.

Attuning the mind for channeling requires more than stillness; it involves building trust in one's inner knowing. As practitioners enter a meditative state, they turn their attention inward, focusing on a gentle inner light that begins to radiate from the heart. This light, which can be visualized as a soft blue or violet glow, represents the connection to the Arcturians. By allowing this light to expand outward, practitioners create an energetic bridge, a pathway that signals readiness to receive messages. This bridge is subtle, felt more than seen, but with each moment of focused intention, it strengthens, allowing a clear line of communication to form.

At the core of channeling lies the ability to discern between one's own thoughts and the guidance being received. This distinction is key, as messages from the Arcturians arrive with a unique quality, often experienced as a calm, steady voice or a profound insight that emerges suddenly yet feels deeply familiar. Practitioners may feel an internal shift, a sense of alignment with something greater, as if the wisdom offered flows from beyond personal understanding. This is the essence of the Arcturian voice—gentle yet powerful, subtle yet unmistakably profound.

To nurture this receptive state, practitioners engage in exercises designed to deepen intuition. One such practice involves sitting quietly and listening to the body, allowing each sensation to come and go without judgment or attachment. By practicing this mindfulness, they develop sensitivity to their inner experience, learning to recognize shifts in energy and presence. As this sensitivity grows, they begin to feel a distinct sense of connection, an energetic invitation that signals the presence of Arcturian guidance. This awareness becomes a compass, helping them navigate the fine line between their own intuition and the wisdom flowing from beyond.

Another essential technique is automatic writing. With pen in hand and mind open, practitioners sit in a meditative state, inviting the Arcturians to communicate through written words. As they relax and let go of expectations, they begin to write freely, without analyzing or editing. Often, the words that appear on the page carry a clarity that surprises them—a clear, concise message that seems to emerge from a space beyond their own thoughts. Over time, this practice becomes a reliable channel, a tangible form through which Arcturian wisdom can be received, recorded, and revisited.

Physical sensations can also accompany channeling experiences. Some practitioners feel a tingling in their hands or a warmth in the heart as the Arcturian presence draws near. These sensations, subtle yet distinct, serve as reminders of the authenticity of the connection. By observing these signals without attaching too much meaning, practitioners allow themselves to remain open, honoring the Arcturian energy without seeking to control it. This openness allows the channel to remain clear, free from personal interpretations that might cloud the message.

As trust in the channeling process deepens, practitioners begin to feel an intimate bond with the Arcturians, a sense of partnership that extends beyond the practice itself. This connection permeates their awareness, guiding them in moments of doubt and offering clarity in times of confusion. Through channeling, the Arcturians become not only teachers but allies, companions on the journey of awakening and growth. The wisdom they offer may come in many forms—a sudden insight, a gentle reassurance, or a vision that speaks to the heart's deepest longings.

This practice requires patience and humility, as the path of channeling is one of gradual refinement. Each session brings a new level of awareness, a deeper understanding of how to open oneself without expectation, allowing the Arcturian energy to flow freely. For those dedicated to this journey, channeling becomes a transformative experience, a direct line to a higher consciousness that illuminates both the inner and outer landscapes of life.

Through these practices, practitioners discover that channeling is more than receiving messages; it is an act of co-creation, a blending of energies that brings wisdom, healing, and insight into the human experience. With each encounter, they step further into a relationship with the Arcturians, cultivating a connection that transcends words and touches the soul.

As the path of Arcturian channeling unfolds, the connection deepens, drawing practitioners further into a practice of refinement and discernment. Each session brings unique experiences, often carrying subtle nuances that must be observed with patience and a steady heart. Beyond simply opening oneself to Arcturian messages, practitioners learn to cultivate clarity, differentiating these messages from the whisper of their own mind. Developing this clarity requires a heightened sensitivity to both internal and external energies—a sensitivity that forms the foundation for a channel that is both authentic and precise.

One of the most effective practices for achieving this precision is focused breathing. Through mindful breathwork, practitioners create an inner stillness, allowing them to reach a level of presence where they can perceive the slightest energetic shifts. As they inhale deeply and exhale slowly, they imagine their breath as a gentle stream that washes through their mind and body, clearing away residual thoughts and preparing them to receive. By connecting each breath with the intention of attuning to Arcturian energy, practitioners ground themselves in the present, creating a field of receptive calm. This breathing practice becomes an anchor, enabling them to remain centered, regardless of what messages may come.

To further enhance discernment, practitioners engage in specific exercises to distinguish Arcturian messages from intuition. One such exercise involves tuning into a question or intention and allowing time for a response to emerge naturally. Practitioners close their eyes, hold the question in their awareness, and sit in silence, observing any sensations, images, or thoughts that arise. By practicing this stillness, they begin to sense the unique quality of Arcturian communication—messages that come from beyond their personal thought stream, carrying a feeling of clarity, calm, and consistency. This process teaches them to recognize the distinct resonance of an Arcturian message, a feeling that often defies words but settles in the heart with certainty.

Another valuable technique in this refinement is voice channeling. Practitioners enter a meditative state, inviting the Arcturian presence, and speak aloud, allowing the messages to flow without interruption or self-judgment. This method allows the energy to move through them in a continuous flow, bypassing mental filters and enabling a direct expression of the guidance. With practice, voice channeling becomes a powerful tool, as it allows the Arcturian messages to take form in real-time, preserving the essence of each word and insight. By recording these sessions, practitioners can later review the messages, allowing them to reflect on the experience with an objective mind, gaining greater insight into the nuances of the Arcturian guidance.

To maintain energetic stability, grounding exercises are essential. Channeling, especially at deeper levels, can create a heightened sensitivity that may leave practitioners feeling ungrounded or lightheaded. Visualizing roots extending from their feet into the earth, they anchor themselves, drawing upon Earth's steadying energy to restore balance. This practice, done after each channeling session, helps reintegrate their energy into the physical realm, creating a sense of wholeness and allowing them to carry the Arcturian messages with a grounded clarity. Grounding is not only a protective measure but also a reminder that channeling exists to benefit both spiritual and earthly dimensions, harmonizing both in the practitioner's experience.

In moments when the messages seem complex or abstract, visualization aids in interpreting the Arcturian guidance. Practitioners may receive symbols, colors, or scenes that initially seem unrelated to their questions. By visualizing these elements in detail and exploring their emotional resonance, they begin to decipher the meanings hidden within. These symbols often carry layers of insight, bridging the gap between words and direct knowing. Practitioners find that the Arcturians communicate not only through concepts but through impressions that bypass the intellect, connecting directly with their inner wisdom.

With each session, a relationship of trust and familiarity deepens. Practitioners become attuned to the specific ways in which Arcturian energy interacts with their own, recognizing that the flow of communication is a living experience, one that shifts and evolves. They may find that the Arcturian messages begin to touch on themes relevant not only to their own life but to collective questions of healing, compassion, and transformation. This shift reflects the Arcturian emphasis on unity consciousness, a reminder that the journey of one is intimately connected to the journey of all.

In these deeper stages of channeling, practitioners often feel a call to share the wisdom they receive, whether through writing, speaking, or simply living by example. The Arcturians, in their quiet and compassionate guidance, encourage this sharing, as each message holds potential to inspire and uplift others. Yet, they also stress the importance of humility and respect for the free will of others. Practitioners are reminded that the purpose of channeling is not to impose wisdom but to offer it as a gift, allowing each person to receive as they feel called. This balanced approach reinforces the Arcturian values of love and non-interference, honoring the individuality of each soul.

With dedication, practitioners find that their channeling practice becomes a sacred dialogue, an ongoing relationship of learning and sharing, receiving and giving. The Arcturian presence is felt not as an external authority but as a companion on the journey, a wise and gentle guide that supports each step toward inner harmony and expanded awareness. Through this practice, practitioners deepen their understanding of themselves, the Arcturians, and the vast, interconnected web of consciousness that unites all beings.

Chapter 5
Self-Healing

In the heart of the Arcturian journey lies the practice of self-healing—a transformative process that allows individuals to access the natural reservoirs of balance and restoration that exist within. The Arcturians, known for their compassionate approach to human evolution, guide practitioners to develop a profound understanding of the self, viewing each challenge, emotion, and experience as a vital part of personal healing.

Self-healing begins with the understanding that the body and mind are interconnected fields of energy, each influencing the other. Physical ailments, emotional wounds, and mental unrest leave imprints in one's energy field, affecting the flow of vitality and clarity. Visualizations serve as powerful tools to address these imprints, allowing practitioners to consciously channel healing energy to areas that feel blocked or out of balance. By visualizing light, symbols, or colors, they create an energetic blueprint that guides the body and mind toward a state of alignment and well-being.

One effective visualization involves envisioning a soft, radiant light entering the body through the crown of the head, gradually filling every cell with warmth and calm. Practitioners may choose colors intuitively, letting each hue reflect a healing intention—perhaps green for renewal, blue for peace, or pink for compassion. As they hold this image, they sense the light moving to areas that feel tense or heavy, dissolving blockages and restoring a natural flow of energy. This practice brings them into a space of surrender, where they feel the gentle touch of Arcturian presence supporting their healing journey.

Another core aspect of Arcturian self-healing is the use of energy symbols. These symbols, often perceived as geometric forms or patterns, serve as focal points for directing energy. Practitioners may visualize these symbols above or around areas of the body that require healing, imagining them as vessels through which Arcturian energy flows. The symbol of a simple, radiant sphere, for instance, can represent wholeness, and when placed over the heart, it encourages the release of stored emotions, inviting a sense of peace. The sacred geometry within these symbols resonates with the subtle structures of the human energy field, creating harmony and coherence on a deep level.

Guided by Arcturian insights, practitioners learn that healing is not a forceful act but a process of allowing, of creating space within oneself for energy to flow freely and naturally. They realize that, at its core, healing is the art of coming into alignment with the truth of who they are—a being of light capable of transformation. As they practice self-healing, they begin to sense layers of themselves that may have been hidden, parts of their mind or emotions that call for compassion and release. This awareness deepens their self-connection, bringing insight into the sources of their challenges and allowing them to address these sources with love.

Breathwork plays a complementary role in self-healing, as the breath becomes both a vehicle and a guide, carrying Arcturian energy into each cell and thought. Practitioners focus on inhaling deeply, imagining the breath as a stream of light that enters with healing intent. With each exhale, they visualize any tension, worry, or discomfort leaving their body, as if released by the gentle tide of the breath. Over time, this practice reveals itself as a powerful rhythm of renewal, grounding the mind and balancing the energy field, making room for Arcturian healing energies to work with ease.

For those who feel called to further strengthen their self-healing practice, daily rituals offer a structure that nurtures this process. Practitioners might begin each day by setting an intention for healing, whether it is a specific focus on an area of physical discomfort or a general sense of peace and balance. This intention becomes a thread that weaves through the day, reminding them to stay aware of their thoughts, actions, and feelings. At night, a brief visualization of cleansing light can help release any energies accumulated throughout the day, creating a sense of closure and peace before sleep.

The Arcturians view healing as a return to one's natural state of balance, an invitation to recognize and embody one's wholeness. Through the practices of visualization, symbols, and breath, practitioners cultivate an inner space where Arcturian energy can flow freely, illuminating and healing. Self-healing becomes a sacred act, a journey to rediscover one's own light and embrace each part of the self with compassion and love.

Self-healing unfolds as an evolving journey, a path that deepens with each step into self-awareness and Arcturian alignment. Practitioners come to understand that healing is not only about addressing discomfort but is an art of nurturing the whole self—a journey that embraces every thought, feeling, and experience. As they move further into this practice, the focus shifts to creating a personalized healing plan, one that weaves self-healing into the rhythm of daily life. This plan serves as both a compass and a sanctuary, guiding practitioners through practices that empower inner transformation.

A foundational element of a self-healing plan involves setting clear intentions that resonate with the practitioner's inner truth. Intentions function as energy markers, focal points that remind practitioners of the essence they are inviting into their lives—balance, courage, compassion, or whatever resonates most deeply. By aligning intentions with Arcturian energy, they begin to bring a focused clarity to the healing process, allowing this energy to flow seamlessly into each practice and guiding them toward deeper healing and self-understanding. These intentions are like seeds planted within the heart, growing steadily and aligning with the Arcturian frequency.

To support this personalized plan, practitioners integrate visualization exercises as daily rituals. One powerful practice involves creating a healing sanctuary within the mind, a place that can be returned to at any time for renewal and alignment. In this sanctuary, practitioners envision a peaceful, sacred space filled with light, where they invite the Arcturian presence to join them. By returning to this sanctuary regularly, they create a stable energetic environment that nurtures ongoing healing and strengthens the bond with Arcturian energy. This inner space becomes a refuge, a place where they feel empowered to release tension and embrace balance.

In addition to visualizations, symbols play an important role in the daily healing plan. Practitioners may select a personal symbol—whether a simple circle, a star, or an intricate geometric pattern—that represents a specific aspect of healing or growth. This symbol can be drawn on paper, visualized in meditation, or even worn as a reminder of their healing intentions. When focused upon, the symbol activates a flow of energy, acting as a bridge that channels Arcturian light into the practitioner's being, bringing healing to any areas of life where balance is needed. The symbol grows with them, reflecting their inner evolution and reinforcing their intentions.

Breathwork further grounds the healing plan, offering a consistent and gentle method of energy cleansing and restoration. Practitioners may choose specific breathing techniques that resonate with their personal rhythm, such as the four-part breath, in which they inhale, hold, exhale, and pause. With each cycle, they visualize light moving in and out, releasing any residual energies and drawing in clarity. This breathing practice reinforces stability, connecting them with the present moment and deepening the Arcturian alignment in a simple yet powerful way. Over time, this breathwork becomes a natural rhythm, a tool for healing that remains with them in all situations.

The healing plan also incorporates mindful reflection, a practice of observing one's emotions and thoughts with compassion and curiosity. Practitioners are encouraged to reflect upon their experiences, noticing patterns, triggers, and areas that feel resistant to healing. By approaching these insights without judgment, they learn to embrace each part of themselves with understanding. This reflection becomes a dialogue between the conscious mind and the Arcturian presence, where moments of clarity often arise. The Arcturian guidance, subtle yet steady, supports practitioners in seeing these patterns not as obstacles but as opportunities for transformation.

Rituals of gratitude and affirmation bring a sense of closure to each day, fostering a healing cycle that extends beyond specific practices. Practitioners end their day by acknowledging any progress, no matter how small, expressing gratitude for the energy and insights received. This ritual of gratitude reinforces a positive connection with the self-healing process, a recognition of the journey's unfolding nature. Affirmations, spoken in a quiet and mindful tone, serve as final reflections for the day. Phrases like "I am open to healing" or "I embrace my path with trust" resonate with the intention set and align the practitioner's energy for rest and renewal.

As practitioners immerse themselves in their self-healing plan, they find that this commitment transforms their daily experiences. Over time, they sense a renewed inner strength, an ability to meet life with a calm that comes from deeper self-awareness and alignment with Arcturian wisdom. This ongoing practice of self-healing opens doors to insights and personal evolution that were previously unseen. The journey grows with them, responding to the nuances of their lives, while the practices become second nature—a steady rhythm guiding them toward wholeness.

This plan becomes a lived experience, a daily return to one's own light, strengthened by the compassionate presence of the Arcturians. Self-healing is no longer just a practice; it is a return to inner truth, a path that brings forth the hidden reserves of resilience, love, and clarity that lie within each heart. Through each visualization, each symbol, and each breath, practitioners come to recognize that the power of healing rests within, nourished by the steady light of Arcturian connection.

Chapter 6
Healing for Others

Healing, when extended to others, becomes a journey of compassion, a practice that goes beyond self-transformation and reaches into the shared fields of human connection. The Arcturians teach that to offer healing to others is to act as a conduit for love, wisdom, and energy, allowing practitioners to assist those around them in restoring balance and harmony within their lives. This practice requires awareness, empathy, and a profound respect for the free will of each individual, as well as an understanding of the unique responsibility involved in channeling healing energy for another.

The foundation of healing for others begins with intention and ethics. Practitioners align themselves with a sincere desire to aid others without attachment to personal outcomes. They understand that healing must respect the integrity and boundaries of the recipient, acknowledging that each person's journey is unique and cannot be forced or manipulated. Practitioners hold a clear intention to serve as a vessel, not as the source of the healing. This clarity of intention creates a protected, compassionate environment in which energy flows freely, guided by the wisdom of the Arcturians and the innate intelligence of the universe.

To prepare for this work, practitioners begin with grounding exercises that center their own energy, stabilizing their field before engaging with another's. They envision roots extending from their feet into the earth, drawing in a steady, grounding energy that provides resilience and clarity. This grounding practice becomes a point of stability that holds them present and receptive, preventing them from absorbing energies that do not belong to them. In this grounded state, they can more effectively channel Arcturian energy, creating a clear line between their own energy field and that of the recipient.

The practice of directed channeling is central to healing for others. Practitioners enter a meditative state, attuning their energy to the Arcturian frequency, allowing themselves to be filled with light. Once attuned, they visualize a gentle stream of energy flowing from their heart or hands to the recipient. This energy, often visualized as a soft blue or violet light, is intended to flow without interference, guided solely by the needs and receptivity of the person receiving it. The practitioner remains a channel, observing the flow of energy with sensitivity and detachment, trusting that the Arcturian presence knows how best to direct the healing process.

A key aspect of directed healing involves the technique of visualization. Practitioners may visualize the recipient enveloped in light, imagining areas of imbalance being gently bathed in healing energy. This visualization acts as a bridge, guiding the energy to specific areas that need support without imposing force or control. Practitioners focus on an image of wholeness and balance, envisioning the recipient's energy field as vibrant and aligned. Through this image, they set an intention for harmony, allowing the Arcturian energy to fill any spaces where imbalance or discomfort may reside, thus inviting a state of equilibrium.

Another essential tool in this process is empathy. Practitioners open their hearts, cultivating a compassionate presence that resonates with the recipient's experience. This empathy is not about absorbing the other's emotions or energy but about offering a space where they feel seen and supported. Through this resonance, practitioners foster a sense of peace and safety that enhances the healing experience. By holding a space of non-judgmental awareness, they allow the recipient to open themselves to the healing process fully, trusting that they are held in a field of genuine care.

As practitioners work with these techniques, they remain mindful of the importance of energetic boundaries. Healing for others can lead to an energetic exchange, and without proper boundaries, there is a risk of absorbing energies that may disrupt the practitioner's field. To protect themselves, practitioners visualize an energy shield surrounding them, a barrier of light that allows only positive, healing energies to pass through. This shield creates a clear line of separation, ensuring that each person's energy remains distinct while allowing the Arcturian frequency to flow freely between them.

At the conclusion of each session, practitioners engage in a gentle closure practice. They take a few moments to express gratitude for the Arcturian guidance, releasing any lingering energy and reaffirming the boundaries of their own field. They might visualize the recipient's energy field as complete and sovereign, allowing them to integrate the healing in their own time and way. This process of closure honors the journey of both the practitioner and recipient, ensuring that each leaves the session feeling grounded and balanced.

In offering healing to others, practitioners learn that they are not simply performing an action; they are embodying a path of service, one that enhances their connection to the Arcturian presence and strengthens their own inner growth. Each session becomes an opportunity to witness the interconnected nature of all beings, deepening their understanding of compassion, empathy, and the profound power of healing energy. Through these practices, healing extends beyond the personal and into the shared, creating a ripple of transformation that touches every life it encounters.

As practitioners grow in their capacity to channel healing energy, their understanding of its potential deepens. Offering Arcturian healing to others becomes not only a practice of energy transmission but a profound act of co-creation, where each session is a unique experience shaped by the needs, openness, and energetic state of the recipient.

Hand positioning becomes a powerful tool in this phase, directing energy with precision to areas that call for healing. Practitioners begin by holding their hands a few inches above the recipient's body, tuning into their intuition to feel where energy might be needed. They may sense warmth, tingling, or a subtle pull that guides them to certain areas. Starting at the crown and moving downward, they allow their hands to hover, resting at each energy center to offer balance and alignment. This hand positioning allows Arcturian energy to flow naturally to points of tension or stagnation, fostering an environment where the recipient's own energy can begin to harmonize.

During this practice, practitioners use visualization to strengthen the flow of healing energy. They may imagine a stream of light, often a gentle blue or violet, flowing from their hands, enveloping the recipient. This light is envisioned as soft and radiant, touching each energy center and encouraging any blockages to dissolve naturally. For deeper healing, practitioners visualize the light moving in spirals or waves, a fluid motion that resonates with the Arcturian frequency, allowing the energy to reach beyond physical limitations and into emotional or spiritual layers. This visualization guides the healing energy with precision, supporting the recipient's unique needs without imposing specific outcomes.

The use of breath complements hand positioning and visualization, creating a rhythm that helps practitioners maintain focus and deepen their connection with the recipient. With each inhale, they gather energy, feeling it rise from within and pool in their hands. As they exhale, they release this energy, allowing it to flow through their hands into the recipient's field. This breathing practice creates a calm, steady rhythm, aligning both practitioner and recipient in a shared state of openness and peace. Each breath becomes an expression of intention, reinforcing the focus and strength of the healing energy without disrupting the natural flow.

Practitioners also engage the power of intention to support the healing process. Each healing session begins with a moment of silent affirmation, setting the purpose for the energy being offered. This intention may be as simple as "May this energy bring peace and balance," creating a clear resonance that shapes the energy field. By holding this intention throughout the session, practitioners reinforce a protective and compassionate space that honors the recipient's free will and respects their journey. The intention serves as a beacon, a guiding light that aligns the session with Arcturian wisdom, ensuring the energy flows in harmony with the recipient's highest good.

Practitioners find that in certain cases, guided visualizations may support the recipient's engagement in the healing process. They may gently suggest that the recipient visualize a place of peace within themselves, encouraging them to release tension or mental resistance. This co-creative approach helps the recipient take an active role in their healing, fostering a sense of empowerment and agency. The practitioner's role becomes one of facilitator, guiding the recipient to access their own healing potential, reinforcing the connection between mind, body, and spirit.

The practice of closure holds a special importance in these sessions. Once the energy work is complete, practitioners take a few moments to ground both themselves and the recipient. They may visualize a gentle seal over the recipient's energy field, a protective layer that allows the healing energy to settle and integrate. Practitioners express gratitude, acknowledging the presence of Arcturian guidance and releasing any residual energy from their own field. This moment of closure ensures that both the practitioner and recipient leave the session feeling grounded, complete, and at peace.

As practitioners continue to offer healing to others, they find that each session brings unique insights and experiences. Each act of healing serves as a mirror, reflecting back lessons in compassion, empathy, and humility. The experience deepens their connection with the Arcturian presence, revealing that healing is as much about their own growth as it is about serving others. Through these practices, they come to see healing as a sacred exchange, one that transcends words and touches the core of both giver and receiver, honoring the journey of both in the unfolding of light and balance.

Chapter 7
Expansion of Consciousness

The journey toward expanded consciousness is an invitation to explore realms within and beyond the self, opening the doors of perception to dimensions often unseen yet profoundly real. The Arcturians, masters of multidimensional wisdom, guide practitioners in developing this awareness, inviting them to step beyond the confines of ordinary experience and into a state of spiritual insight. Through specific practices and meditations, practitioners begin to access a deeper understanding of their own consciousness, exploring their place within the vast tapestry of existence, and touching aspects of their being that resonate with the boundless frequencies of the universe.

Practitioners start with an understanding of consciousness as a spectrum, one that extends from ordinary waking awareness into states that are subtle, profound, and transformative. They are encouraged to perceive their mind as a vessel capable of traveling beyond its habitual boundaries, able to expand and explore dimensions of thought, feeling, and intuition that remain hidden in the ordinary. This perspective opens the way for deeper experiences, inviting them to connect with an awareness that transcends the individual, touching the collective consciousness and even the wisdom of higher realms.

Meditation becomes a primary tool for this expansion. Practitioners engage in meditative practices designed to move them beyond mental chatter, creating a state of stillness where insight arises naturally. The Arcturians guide them in focusing on the breath, allowing it to become slow and rhythmic, bringing them into a relaxed state where the mind is open yet clear. From this quiet space, practitioners may feel an expanded awareness, a sense of moving beyond the personal into a field of collective presence where thoughts, emotions, and sensations blend into a unified flow. In this meditative state, they begin to perceive life from a perspective that is timeless, spacious, and deeply connected.

Another essential practice for expanding consciousness involves exploring the energy centers, or chakras, beyond their physical dimensions. Practitioners begin by focusing on each chakra, visualizing it as a portal not only to inner aspects of the self but as an opening into greater dimensions of consciousness. By aligning their awareness with the chakras in meditation, they sense these energy centers as points of resonance, each one vibrating in harmony with a larger field of spiritual insight. The third eye and crown chakras, in particular, are encouraged to open, as these centers are linked to intuition and universal connection, bridging the inner world with realms beyond ordinary perception.

To deepen this awareness, practitioners are guided to use visualizations that expand their perception of space and time. One powerful exercise is to visualize themselves surrounded by an infinite field of stars, a space that extends in all directions without limit. As they visualize this vastness, they sense their consciousness merging with the space around them, feeling themselves both as an individual presence and as part of a boundless universe. This dual awareness—a sense of self that exists within the all-encompassing unity of creation—begins to dissolve the ego's limitations, opening practitioners to a perspective that is both vast and profoundly personal.

Practices involving sound, such as chanting or listening to harmonic frequencies, also support the expansion of consciousness. Sound carries vibrations that resonate deeply within the mind and body, helping practitioners access meditative states where higher awareness emerges naturally. By focusing on specific tones or chants, practitioners allow sound to guide them into expanded states of being, aligning their own energy with frequencies that are said to resonate with the Arcturians' vibrational field. In these states, practitioners may experience visions, sensations, or insights that carry a sense of wisdom and connection to something beyond themselves.

Throughout this process, grounding remains essential. Expansion of consciousness, especially into higher realms, requires balance. Practitioners engage in grounding exercises after each session, visualizing roots that extend from their feet into the earth, drawing in stabilizing energy. This practice ensures that even as they touch realms beyond the ordinary, they remain fully connected to their physical being, anchoring their experiences in the body so that insights can be integrated into daily life. This balance between expansion and grounding allows practitioners to explore consciousness with safety, bringing back the wisdom they encounter to enrich their inner and outer worlds.

As practitioners expand their awareness, they begin to sense the interconnectedness of all things, recognizing themselves as both distinct and intimately woven into the fabric of the universe. The Arcturian presence guides them gently through these realizations, supporting them in each step toward a consciousness that embraces unity, compassion, and insight. The journey becomes a passage into a truth that is both personal and universal, an awareness that transforms every perception, opening a path to spiritual insight and a deeper understanding of the self as part of a much greater whole.

As the journey of expanding consciousness deepens, practitioners come to recognize consciousness itself as a limitless field, one that unfolds layer by layer as they attune to higher frequencies. With each experience, they learn to move beyond ordinary perception, connecting more fully with the Arcturian presence and the wisdom within.

To reach these expanded states, practitioners begin with a refined form of meditation that focuses on elevated sensory awareness. They are encouraged to sit in silence, closing their eyes and breathing steadily, letting each sense open gently, beyond the physical, into the subtle realms. Through this heightened awareness, they begin to perceive the nuances of energy—sensations, colors, or vibrations that exist beyond normal sight or sound. Each inhale draws in clarity, each exhale releases attachment to what is familiar, inviting the mind to explore the vastness that lies within.

Visualizations offer another path to these higher states, taking practitioners deeper into the realms of multidimensional perception. One potent technique involves visualizing a pillar of light extending from above, flowing through the crown chakra and down to the earth. This pillar becomes a channel of cosmic energy, a bridge that connects them with Arcturian wisdom and aligns them with universal consciousness. As practitioners imagine themselves bathed in this light, they sense their awareness expanding, opening to insights that emerge not as thoughts but as a knowing—a direct understanding that transcends words.

In these states, practitioners often experience what the Arcturians describe as "spiritual resonance"—a feeling of unity and harmony that arises when consciousness attunes to the frequencies of the cosmos. This resonance brings a profound sense of belonging, as if each practitioner is a vital note in a greater symphony. In this elevated state, they begin to access knowledge that feels timeless, drawn from a source beyond individual experience. This resonance is not just a momentary experience; it becomes a guide, a vibrational compass that aligns each thought, feeling, and action with the wisdom of the higher self.

Balancing these elevated states with daily life requires deliberate practices that anchor these insights into practical actions. Practitioners are encouraged to keep a journal, recording not just their experiences in meditation but also the reflections and insights that arise from these expanded states. Writing serves as a bridge, bringing abstract wisdom into concrete understanding. Each entry becomes a moment of integration, a way of weaving spiritual insight into the fabric of daily awareness, transforming moments of clarity into lifelong growth.

Breathing practices designed for sustained consciousness expansion also support this process. By practicing rhythmic breathing—such as the four-part breath, where practitioners inhale, hold, exhale, and pause—they create a steady flow of energy that fosters balance. This breathing sequence serves as a grounding rhythm, allowing them to access elevated states while maintaining a connection to the physical body. Each breath cycle brings them closer to a state of inner equilibrium, where the vastness of expanded consciousness coexists with the simplicity of grounded presence.

Practitioners are also guided to develop what the Arcturians refer to as "reflective stillness"—a quiet, inner awareness that allows each experience of expanded consciousness to deepen without mental analysis. By cultivating reflective stillness, practitioners release the need to interpret or categorize their experiences, allowing insights to settle naturally, like a lake returning to calm after a ripple. This stillness becomes a sanctuary, a state of awareness where the depth of spiritual experience can be absorbed without distortion, allowing wisdom to emerge in its purest form.

As practitioners master these techniques, they experience a shift in perception, sensing reality not as a series of separate events but as a fluid, interconnected whole. They begin to see beyond appearances, recognizing the energy and consciousness that underlie all things. This expanded awareness fosters compassion, empathy, and a profound sense of unity with others, as they come to understand that every individual, every experience, is a reflection of the same universal light. The teachings of the Arcturians illuminate this path, guiding practitioners to embrace consciousness as an endless journey, one where each insight leads to a new level of understanding.

Through these practices, the expanded states of awareness become more than isolated experiences—they transform into a way of being. Practitioners find themselves returning to this consciousness even in ordinary moments, experiencing life with an openness and clarity that touches every thought and action. The journey to higher states of awareness becomes a continual unfolding, a way to move through life in alignment with the rhythms of the cosmos, embracing each moment as part of an endless, evolving dance of consciousness.

Chapter 8
Higher Dimensions

As practitioners move into the exploration of higher dimensions, they enter a realm where ordinary boundaries of time, space, and form dissolve into expansive waves of energy and consciousness. The Arcturians, beings of elevated vibration, exist within these higher-dimensional frequencies, residing in planes of awareness that extend beyond the material world. Connecting with these dimensions requires an openness to experience energies and insights beyond human perception, touching aspects of consciousness that resonate with universal wisdom and the profound stillness of existence.

The journey into higher dimensions begins with an understanding of these planes not as distant realms but as levels of consciousness accessible through intention, practice, and energetic alignment. Practitioners learn that the human energy field can resonate with multiple dimensions, each carrying a unique vibrational signature. The first step in accessing these realms is to attune to their frequency, raising one's own energy by cultivating purity of thought, clarity of intention, and openness of heart. Through this attunement, practitioners align themselves with the Arcturian frequency, tuning into a space where connection with higher dimensions becomes a lived reality.

Meditation practices focused on elevation guide practitioners toward these higher states. In these meditations, they visualize themselves as part of a vast, luminous field, free from the limitations of the physical world. They may picture themselves surrounded by an expansive blue or violet light, colors that resonate with the Arcturian frequency, allowing this light to gently raise their vibration. Each breath deepens this state, creating a calm openness that lifts them beyond daily awareness, into realms where the energies feel lighter, finer, and filled with profound wisdom. This visualization, combined with breathing, serves as a doorway, guiding the mind and spirit into the subtle yet powerful frequency of higher dimensions.

A key element in this exploration is learning to perceive and differentiate between the vibrational levels of these dimensions. The Arcturians suggest that higher dimensions are not defined by physical distance but by resonance—a natural alignment of energies that allows consciousness to rise and merge with these planes. Practitioners may initially feel this as a shift in awareness, a sensation of expansiveness, or a subtle tingling that signals alignment. As they deepen into these frequencies, they become more attuned to the specific qualities of each dimensional field, sensing the unique texture of Arcturian presence and the peace that pervades these spaces.

To facilitate entry into these realms, practitioners often work with symbols or sacred geometry. Visualizing symbols such as spirals, pyramids, or spheres within their meditation helps to refine their focus and elevate their frequency. Each shape holds a vibrational pattern that resonates with different aspects of the higher dimensions, guiding practitioners into deeper alignment with these energies. The use of these symbols creates an anchor, a subtle yet powerful focal point that helps their consciousness stabilize within these dimensions, allowing the Arcturian connection to deepen and expand.

Sound, too, serves as a bridge to higher dimensions. Tones and frequencies that resonate with the heart and crown chakras support this elevation, allowing practitioners to enter a receptive state where they can perceive higher-dimensional energies more clearly. Singing bowls, tuning forks, or gentle chants create a harmonic resonance, clearing the energy field and preparing the mind for the journey. Practitioners immerse themselves in these sounds, feeling them reverberate through their being, lifting them into a state where the distinction between self and the universe becomes porous and fluid, opening a direct connection with higher realms.

As they become more comfortable with these elevated states, practitioners may experience impressions or visions, glimpses of the energies and forms present in these dimensions. Some perceive colors, patterns, or sensations that carry a unique essence, often accompanied by a profound feeling of peace and unity. These experiences are not simply passive perceptions; they are exchanges, where the practitioner's consciousness merges with the frequency of these realms, touching the Arcturian presence and accessing knowledge that transcends words. This contact fosters a sense of spiritual elevation, an understanding that life is intricately connected to dimensions that hold infinite wisdom and compassion.

Through this journey, practitioners are encouraged to maintain a balance between their exploration and groundedness. As they touch these higher dimensions, grounding practices ensure that they integrate these energies into their daily lives. Visualizing themselves rooted to the earth, feeling the stability of the ground beneath them, allows them to bring these elevated states back into their physical reality. This grounding ensures that the wisdom and energy they receive become part of their inner growth, enriching their perception without destabilizing their everyday awareness.

In connecting with higher dimensions, practitioners find that they are not separate from these realms but an intrinsic part of them. The Arcturians guide them to see that consciousness itself is limitless, capable of reaching into the farthest planes of awareness while remaining fully present. This exploration reveals a truth that transcends form—a realization of unity, a deep and abiding connection to the greater whole of existence. Through each meditation, each symbol, and each sound, they awaken to a consciousness that is boundless, a journey that invites them to return to the heart of the cosmos, where all things are one, and where the light of the Arcturians continues to guide with wisdom and compassion.

As practitioners delve further into the realms of higher dimensions, the journey takes on a new depth. The exploration of these planes becomes an immersive experience, where each meditation and each technique draws them closer to a living connection with the energies of the Arcturians. Moving beyond the introductory practices, practitioners now engage with advanced methods designed to stabilize their consciousness in these higher states, allowing them to receive the profound insights and healing that arise from prolonged contact with higher-dimensional frequencies.

To deepen this contact, practitioners begin with advanced visualization techniques that enhance their ability to perceive and remain aligned with the Arcturian energy field. One such technique involves visualizing themselves within a crystalline chamber of light, a translucent structure that amplifies their vibration and protects their energy as they enter higher dimensions. They see themselves surrounded by facets of radiant crystal, each facet reflecting and enhancing their frequency. This chamber becomes a sacred space where they can feel the presence of higher realms with clarity and ease, each breath drawing them deeper into the Arcturian resonance.

Another powerful practice for stability in these states is focused breathwork, specifically designed to sustain higher awareness. Practitioners are guided to breathe in cycles that match the rhythm of their heart, creating a harmonic flow that unifies body and spirit. With each inhale, they draw in the energy of the higher dimensions, feeling it fill their mind, heart, and energy field. Each exhale releases any residual tension, allowing them to remain open and receptive. This rhythmic breathing not only supports their ability to sustain contact with these realms but also grounds their awareness, ensuring that they can fully integrate the insights received.

In these states, practitioners may also work with mantra repetition to maintain a stable vibration. The Arcturians recommend specific sound syllables—tones that resonate with higher chakras, such as the crown and third eye. These mantras, when repeated slowly and intentionally, create a vibrational anchor, guiding the mind away from distractions and maintaining the alignment needed to stay connected with the higher frequencies. Practitioners feel the resonance of these sounds permeate their being, lifting their consciousness and drawing them into a deeper, more expansive state where Arcturian presence can be directly felt.

The use of sacred geometry becomes an additional tool in these practices, aiding in the navigation of higher-dimensional experiences. Practitioners are encouraged to visualize intricate patterns, such as the flower of life or the Merkaba, surrounding and interconnecting with their energy. These shapes carry their own resonance, creating a structure within the practitioner's field that harmonizes with the Arcturian dimensions. As they focus on these patterns, they find that their awareness naturally aligns with the unique qualities of each dimension, allowing them to perceive with clarity and to stabilize within these elevated states.

During prolonged contact with higher dimensions, practitioners may begin to experience profound shifts in perception. Time may feel fluid, as if the past, present, and future merge into a single moment of awareness. The boundaries of identity soften, allowing a sense of oneness with all beings, with the energies of the cosmos, and with the Arcturian presence itself. These experiences are not merely visions; they are states of understanding that reveal the inherent unity and interconnectivity of all existence. Practitioners often describe these moments as deeply healing, where longstanding emotional or mental barriers dissolve in the light of expanded awareness.

To fully integrate these experiences, grounding techniques become essential. Upon returning from these meditative states, practitioners visualize roots extending deep into the earth, allowing any excess energy to flow downward. This grounding ensures that the elevated vibrations experienced in higher dimensions harmonize with the physical body and mind.

Practitioners may also connect with their physical senses—feeling the texture of objects around them, listening to ambient sounds, or taking slow, deliberate steps. These actions serve to anchor the expansive insights into their everyday lives, creating a bridge between the spiritual and the physical.

Integration also involves reflective practices, where practitioners take time to consider the wisdom they have accessed. Journaling becomes a valuable tool here, as it allows them to capture impressions, images, or feelings that emerged during their journeys into higher dimensions. This reflection helps solidify their experiences, translating abstract insights into actionable understanding. Over time, these reflections reveal patterns, guiding practitioners in their ongoing journey of self-discovery and aligning their actions with the insights gained from these elevated states.

In working with these higher-dimensional practices, practitioners come to realize that these realms are not separate from their own consciousness but an inherent part of it. The Arcturians serve as guides on this journey, helping them to understand that higher-dimensional awareness is not a destination but a state of being, one that can be accessed at any time with the right tools and mindset. Through these practices, practitioners learn to carry the essence of higher-dimensional wisdom within them, transforming their perception of self and reality, and nurturing a path that bridges the infinite with the everyday.

Each session, each meditation, becomes a step toward greater unity and understanding, leading practitioners into a life that resonates with the boundless energy of the cosmos and the wisdom of the Arcturians.

Chapter 9
Personal Transformation

The Arcturian connection, as practitioners begin to understand, is not only a path to higher realms but a catalyst for profound personal transformation. Through this bond, they are guided into a journey of self-discovery and inner refinement, one that unveils layers of potential previously hidden. The Arcturians act as both mentors and mirrors, reflecting the qualities and virtues that lie dormant within, encouraging each individual to step into a truer expression of themselves. This transformation is not sudden or imposed; it unfolds gradually, fueled by practices that deepen self-knowledge and cultivate virtues aligned with the Arcturian way.

A primary focus of this transformative journey is expanding self-awareness. Practitioners are guided to examine their inner world with curiosity and compassion, developing a deeper understanding of their thoughts, emotions, and behaviors. This self-exploration is not about judgment but about observing the patterns and beliefs that shape their experiences. Through meditation and reflection, practitioners begin to identify areas where they feel limited or disconnected from their authentic selves. They learn that transformation starts from within, recognizing that each thought and feeling carries energy that influences their life path.

Practitioners are encouraged to work with introspective meditations, practices that allow them to sit with their experiences, observing without attachment. One such meditation involves visualizing a calm lake, with each thought or feeling appearing as a ripple on its surface. By watching these ripples come and go, they begin to detach from reactions and allow deeper insights to emerge. This process reveals layers of themselves they may have overlooked, helping them understand the underlying motivations and fears that drive their actions. In this stillness, they begin to see that transformation is not about changing who they are but about unveiling their truest self.

Another technique that supports personal transformation is the cultivation of personal virtues. The Arcturians emphasize the development of qualities such as patience, compassion, and humility, as these virtues create a foundation for authentic spiritual growth. Practitioners start by choosing one virtue that resonates with their current journey. They dedicate time each day to contemplate this virtue, bringing it into their awareness and seeking ways to embody it in small, everyday actions. As they practice these virtues, they feel subtle shifts in their energy and perception, sensing a growing alignment with the Arcturian qualities of peace, wisdom, and unity.

To deepen the transformative process, practitioners may work with specific visualizations that support the release of old patterns and the integration of new energies. One powerful visualization involves imagining a gentle light entering through the crown of the head, moving through the entire body and releasing any dense or stagnant energy that no longer serves them. As this light moves downward, it clears away layers of old habits, fears, and limitations, making space for the qualities they wish to cultivate. Practitioners feel themselves become lighter, more open to growth, and ready to welcome the new aspects of themselves that emerge through this practice.

Affirmations play a complementary role in this journey. By repeating simple, clear affirmations, practitioners reinforce their intentions for transformation. Statements like "I am open to growth," "I embrace my true self," or "I am a channel for compassion" serve as gentle reminders, realigning the mind with the spirit's goals. These affirmations, spoken with intention, become seeds planted in the subconscious, supporting a mindset that is open to change and aligned with higher wisdom. Practitioners find that as they repeat these affirmations, they not only shift their thoughts but also their entire energy field, creating a resonance that draws transformative experiences into their lives.

Reflection and journaling provide additional support, helping practitioners to process and integrate the experiences of their journey. Each entry allows them to explore insights, patterns, or breakthroughs, capturing the subtle shifts that may otherwise go unnoticed. This practice becomes a mirror, showing them how they have evolved over time and revealing recurring themes that may need deeper attention. By documenting their journey, they build a narrative of growth that reinforces their commitment to transformation, offering them a tangible reminder of the progress they are making, one step at a time.

Through these practices, practitioners begin to feel a growing sense of wholeness, an alignment with their true nature that reflects the wisdom of the Arcturian presence. The transformation is not a departure from who they are but a return to their most authentic essence. This path reveals a self that is resilient, compassionate, and open to the vastness of life. With each practice, each moment of awareness, they step further into their potential, guided by the light of the Arcturians and the quiet strength that lies within.

The journey of personal transformation becomes a source of empowerment and purpose, awakening a deep connection to the self and to the greater flow of the universe. Practitioners discover that the Arcturian connection is a call not only to explore higher realms but to embody the highest expression of their own being. Through this path, they come to see that transformation is a continuous unfolding—a journey that reveals, layer by layer, the infinite potential that lies within.

As practitioners continue their journey of transformation, the process evolves into a conscious act of co-creation, guided by a deeper relationship with the Arcturian presence. Building upon the initial insights gained through self-awareness and the cultivation of virtues, this next phase introduces the creation of a spiritual plan—a structured yet fluid guide that supports personal growth and integrates Arcturian practices into daily life. The plan serves as a bridge between vision and action, helping practitioners cultivate a life that reflects their highest intentions and resonates with the wisdom they are discovering.

The spiritual plan begins with reflection and setting clear, purposeful goals. Practitioners are encouraged to take time to listen to their inner voice, contemplating areas where they seek growth or healing. By setting intentions that align with their spiritual journey, they create a roadmap that honors their unique path. These goals may be subtle, such as cultivating inner peace or practicing forgiveness, or more specific, like dedicating time to meditation or studying Arcturian teachings. The clarity of purpose provides a foundation for steady growth, helping practitioners remain grounded in their path while allowing room for spontaneous insight and change.

One of the core elements of this plan is the daily integration of practices that reinforce the Arcturian connection. Practitioners establish routines that support both inner stillness and active reflection, such as beginning each day with a brief meditation or a moment of gratitude. These small but consistent practices reinforce their alignment with Arcturian energies, nurturing a steady inner connection that grows more resilient with time. By bringing these practices into their routine, practitioners find that spiritual transformation becomes woven into the fabric of daily life, transforming ordinary moments into opportunities for insight and growth.

To further ground their intentions, practitioners create rituals that mark significant points in their journey. These rituals might involve lighting a candle, reciting an affirmation, or setting aside a space in the home for quiet reflection and meditation. These acts, while simple, serve as anchors that remind them of their commitment to personal transformation. Each ritual becomes a gesture of dedication, an acknowledgment of their growth, and a celebration of the steps taken toward wholeness. Over time, these rituals create an environment that supports and amplifies the transformative energies they are nurturing within.

Journaling continues to play a vital role, offering practitioners a space to reflect upon and document their experiences. Each entry provides insight, allowing them to track patterns and shifts in awareness that occur through the practices they have committed to. Practitioners are encouraged to explore their challenges and breakthroughs, capturing the essence of their journey with honesty and depth. This reflective process reveals recurring themes, underlying motivations, and areas where healing may still be needed. By journaling, they witness their transformation in real time, deepening their understanding of both their progress and the ongoing work ahead.

As the spiritual plan unfolds, practitioners learn the importance of adaptability. Transformation is a fluid process, and the Arcturian guidance often brings unexpected shifts in perspective. Practitioners are reminded to approach their plan with openness, allowing it to evolve naturally. They may adjust their practices, goals, or routines as they gain clarity, trusting that the journey will lead them toward a fuller understanding of themselves. This flexibility ensures that the plan remains a living document, responsive to the rhythms of life and the insights gained along the way.

Another key element in the spiritual plan is a focus on self-compassion and patience. Practitioners recognize that transformation is an ongoing process, one that unfolds at its own pace. The Arcturians emphasize the importance of kindness toward oneself, encouraging practitioners to release judgment and embrace the present moment with acceptance. When challenges or setbacks arise, they are seen not as failures but as opportunities for greater understanding. This compassionate perspective allows practitioners to navigate their journey with grace, honoring each stage of growth as an essential part of the path.

To deepen their experience of transformation, practitioners are encouraged to share their journey with trusted individuals, whether in a spiritual community, with friends, or through mentorship. Sharing insights and experiences with others creates a sense of connection and mutual support, amplifying the transformative energy of their practices. This act of sharing brings a new layer to their journey, as they witness the universal themes that link all seekers, reinforcing their commitment to personal growth while contributing to the collective journey of those around them.

As the spiritual plan takes root, practitioners begin to sense a profound shift in their inner and outer worlds. The Arcturian connection grows richer, their awareness deepens, and their actions increasingly reflect the virtues they have cultivated. This transformation is not a destination but a continual process, one that unfolds naturally as they align more closely with their true self. Each goal reached and each practice embraced becomes a stepping stone, drawing them into an ever-greater harmony with both the Arcturian presence and the light within.

Through this approach, practitioners come to understand that personal transformation is not about becoming something new but about returning to a place of authenticity and wholeness. The Arcturians serve as gentle guides, reminding them that the path to transformation lies in the simple yet profound journey of becoming who they already are, embracing each moment, and living from the heart.

Chapter 10
Arcturian Meditations

The art of meditation, refined and guided by the Arcturians, serves as a profound gateway for deepening connection and awakening the inner realms. Within these practices, practitioners find a sanctuary—a space where the mind quiets, the heart opens, and the spirit expands into harmony with higher frequencies. Arcturian meditations invite a journey inward, allowing practitioners to experience their own consciousness as both vast and intimate. These meditative techniques, while simple in structure, carry the wisdom of ages and resonate with energies that support healing, insight, and spiritual alignment.

The journey into Arcturian meditation begins with a focus on presence, the act of simply being. Practitioners are encouraged to find a comfortable place where they feel calm and secure, sitting with a relaxed posture and taking gentle, mindful breaths. This initial stillness opens a doorway to heightened awareness, allowing the mind to settle and attune to subtler vibrations. As they breathe, they may sense a gentle shift, as though the atmosphere itself becomes softer and more receptive—a signal that they are entering a state of openness to Arcturian guidance and energy.

One foundational technique involves visualization, a practice that serves as a bridge between the mind and the spirit. Practitioners begin by envisioning a soft, blue light filling the space around them, a color often associated with Arcturian energy. They imagine this light gradually surrounding and entering their body, soothing each cell, calming each thought, and aligning their energy field. This visualization anchors them in a higher frequency, helping them enter a meditative state where they feel both relaxed and alert. With each breath, they draw in this light, sensing it fill their heart and expand outward, creating an aura of peace that surrounds them.

As they deepen into this visualization, practitioners are guided to focus on specific energy centers, or chakras, to enhance their alignment with the Arcturian presence. Beginning with the heart chakra, they visualize a radiant green or pink light expanding from their chest, representing compassion, connection, and harmony. They then move their awareness to the third eye, visualizing a deep indigo light that opens their intuition, preparing their mind to receive insights. These visualizations activate each center, creating a pathway that aligns the practitioner's energy with the Arcturian frequency, setting the stage for a deepened experience.

Another meditation technique involves the practice of silent witnessing. In this approach, practitioners simply observe their thoughts, emotions, and sensations without attachment or analysis. As they sit in silence, they allow each thought to drift by like a cloud, observing it with calm detachment. This witnessing creates a space of pure awareness, where the mind relaxes, allowing the practitioner to access deeper layers of consciousness. In this stillness, they often feel a gentle, comforting presence, as though the Arcturian energy has come forward, filling the space with a calm and loving resonance that supports their meditation.

To support these states of quiet awareness, practitioners may work with mantras. These mantras are often sounds or phrases that resonate with the Arcturian frequency, such as "Om" or "Ah," each repeated softly and rhythmically. This repetition focuses the mind and harmonizes the energy field, bringing the practitioner into alignment with higher realms. With each utterance, they feel their consciousness expanding, their awareness deepening, and their connection to the Arcturian presence growing stronger. The mantra acts as a subtle guide, leading them gently inward, where layers of mind and spirit begin to reveal themselves.

The breath serves as a vital component throughout these meditative practices. Practitioners are encouraged to breathe mindfully, feeling each inhale as a wave of light entering their being and each exhale as a release of tension and thought. This breathing anchors them in the present moment, creating a rhythm that supports both relaxation and awareness. Each breath serves as a reminder of the flow of life, the steady pulse that connects all beings. This mindful breathing becomes a bridge to deeper states, a rhythm that leads them naturally into a place of unity and peace.

As practitioners settle into these meditative practices, they may experience subtle shifts in perception. Colors, shapes, or even symbolic images may appear in their mind's eye, each carrying a personal resonance or insight. These visions, though subtle, often feel deeply familiar, as if they carry a message or understanding from beyond. Practitioners are encouraged to observe these images without judgment, allowing them to emerge and fade naturally, trusting that each one carries a meaning that will become clear with time and reflection.

Through these meditation techniques, practitioners discover that the connection with the Arcturians becomes more tangible, a felt presence that brings healing, clarity, and spiritual support. These moments of stillness reveal layers of consciousness that lie just beyond ordinary perception, a landscape where wisdom and peace abound. The Arcturian meditations guide practitioners gently, helping them discover their own vastness and the subtle energies that connect them to the greater whole. This connection grows with each practice, a steady presence that illuminates the path of spiritual growth and deepened self-awareness.

As practitioners grow familiar with the foundational practices of Arcturian meditation, their journey deepens into techniques that amplify and refine this connection. These advanced meditative practices, enhanced by Arcturian guidance, cultivate an atmosphere of profound stillness, where insights emerge naturally and healing energy flows with precision. In this space, practitioners experience the full resonance of Arcturian presence, guiding them beyond surface consciousness and into a harmonious alignment with higher realms. Each meditation becomes a transformative experience, bringing clarity, balance, and a profound sense of inner unity.

A technique central to this phase involves guided Arcturian visualization, a method that draws practitioners further into meditative depth. Practitioners begin by visualizing themselves in a landscape of peace—a field of soft light, a quiet forest, or a gentle ocean, whichever imagery resonates with their inner stillness. They sense the Arcturian energy surrounding this space, filling it with a palpable presence of peace and wisdom. This visualization not only relaxes the body and mind but serves as a bridge to deeper connection. Practitioners are encouraged to allow this visualization to unfold naturally, trusting that each detail reveals a layer of guidance, enhancing their connection and supporting the flow of insight.

To intensify their experience, practitioners focus on "energy infusion" meditations, where specific areas of the body are visualized as centers of light. They begin by focusing on the heart center, envisioning a soft, radiant glow expanding outward with each breath. This glow fills the chest, bringing warmth and calm to the entire body. From here, they expand the energy to other centers—the crown, where they envision a brilliant light connecting them to the cosmos, and the third eye, where a serene light opens intuition and inner vision. Through these focused energy infusions, practitioners create a cohesive field that aligns with the Arcturian frequency, each center resonating with clarity and strength.

Sound becomes a profound ally in this phase of meditation. Practitioners incorporate harmonic tones or chanting, selecting sounds that resonate with higher chakras and elevate their energy field. Whether through a soft chant or the tones of singing bowls, these sounds resonate with the subtle frequencies of the Arcturian dimensions, creating a bridge that supports the flow of energy. Practitioners allow each sound to ripple through their being, moving them beyond the physical into the realms of pure consciousness. This resonance creates an environment where meditation becomes seamless, a state of natural flow where insight and presence merge into one.

Practitioners are guided to engage in what the Arcturians call "inner field attunement"—a practice of scanning the energy field to identify areas of tension, imbalance, or sensitivity. They do this by shifting their awareness gently through each layer of their energy, observing any sensations that arise with calm curiosity. As they identify areas that feel heavy or blocked, they visualize these spaces infused with light, inviting the Arcturian presence to restore harmony. This attunement fosters self-awareness, showing practitioners the subtle interconnections within their being and allowing the healing energy to move precisely where it is needed.

In addition to visualization and sound, practitioners work with expanded breathing practices. The Arcturians encourage a specific breathing pattern for deepened alignment, called the "three-part breath." Here, practitioners inhale in three stages—filling the lower lungs, the middle chest, and then the upper chest before exhaling smoothly. This breath sequence brings a calm focus, harmonizing the physical with the subtle energy bodies, creating a unified flow that enhances both relaxation and receptivity. As they breathe in this rhythm, practitioners feel themselves sink into a deeper meditative state, where insights and healing emerge effortlessly.

During these expanded states, practitioners often experience shifts in awareness, as if boundaries between their consciousness and the universe dissolve. Colors, symbols, or impressions may emerge—visuals that feel deeply personal, resonating with aspects of their inner journey. Practitioners observe these impressions without attachment, trusting that each one carries meaning that will unfold in time. These moments of open perception are not just visual; they are energetic impressions, direct communications from the Arcturian presence that resonate beyond words, touching the soul with guidance that is felt rather than understood.

As each session concludes, grounding becomes a central practice to integrate the energies and insights received. Practitioners visualize roots extending from their feet deep into the earth, feeling the stability and strength of the ground beneath them. This grounding ensures that the elevated states experienced in meditation settle harmoniously within the physical self. They then take a few deep breaths, returning their awareness to the present moment, gently closing the meditative state. Through this grounding, they integrate the healing and insights of the Arcturian meditation, carrying its essence into daily life with calm focus and clarity.

These advanced Arcturian meditations cultivate a refined awareness that reaches beyond the surface of consciousness. Practitioners begin to sense their own energy field as interconnected with the greater flow of life, experiencing a unity that transcends individuality. The Arcturian presence, with each session, becomes a subtle, steady guide, illuminating their path of spiritual growth and self-discovery. As practitioners continue these meditations, they find themselves not merely connecting with Arcturian wisdom but embodying it, bringing the insights of higher realms into each moment with grace and purpose.

Chapter 11
Advanced Energy Healing

As practitioners evolve in their Arcturian journey, their understanding of energy healing reaches a profound level of depth. In this advanced phase, Arcturian teachings reveal intricate techniques that move beyond basic healing, allowing practitioners to explore the subtleties of resonance and energetic manipulation.

One of the key elements of advanced Arcturian healing is resonance. Practitioners learn that resonance is the harmonious vibration created when their energy field aligns perfectly with that of the recipient or with a specific intention. By fine-tuning their awareness, practitioners begin to feel the subtle shifts and movements within energy fields, allowing them to identify areas of imbalance with precision. They approach this process with deep presence, sensing the unique vibrational "signature" of each area. This attuned listening creates a natural resonance, allowing the energy field to harmonize and begin the healing process without force, guided purely by alignment.

To engage more fully in this resonance, practitioners employ techniques of intentional energy manipulation. Visualization serves as a powerful tool, enabling practitioners to guide energy flows with precision. One technique involves visualizing currents of light, often appearing as soft, flowing colors, entering areas that need attention. Practitioners may envision this light as a gentle stream or a spiral, moving with a steady rhythm that mirrors the natural cycles of life. By focusing their intent on these currents, they direct the Arcturian energy with clarity, infusing areas of stagnation or blockages with revitalizing frequencies. This flow is not imposed but offered, allowing the recipient's own energy field to absorb and integrate it at its own pace.

Another technique in advanced energy healing is the practice of layered energy work. Practitioners learn to recognize that healing often requires working through multiple layers of the body and spirit—beginning with the physical, moving into the emotional, mental, and eventually, spiritual levels. To address these layers, practitioners move through each one systematically, visualizing the energy as they descend into each depth. As they work through these layers, they may experience subtle shifts, sensing when one layer releases tension or clears, allowing them to move deeper. This layered approach respects the complexity of healing, acknowledging that true transformation often involves addressing energies from multiple dimensions of experience.

The Arcturians also guide practitioners in the use of specific energy patterns, shapes, or symbols that amplify and direct healing. Practitioners are encouraged to visualize symbols that resonate with the recipient's energy field, such as spirals for gentle release, triangles for alignment, or circles for protection and grounding. These symbols act as carriers of specific frequencies, creating a vibrational structure that enhances the healing process. By visualizing these forms over or around areas in need of healing, practitioners provide a stable framework that helps guide the recipient's energy field back into balance.

Breathwork, already familiar in previous practices, becomes even more precise in this phase, with breathing sequences crafted to sustain and focus the healer's energy. Practitioners use the "pulse breath" technique, inhaling deeply to gather energy and exhaling with a focused intent, directing the breath toward specific points or areas. Each pulse breath infuses the targeted area with fresh energy, encouraging the release of blockages. This rhythmic breathing grounds the practitioner's own energy field, ensuring that the healing flow remains strong and uninterrupted. Practitioners feel the breath become a part of the energy itself, a vessel for Arcturian light that reaches deep into the layers being healed.

Throughout these practices, grounding remains essential, ensuring that both practitioner and recipient remain balanced and stable. Practitioners ground themselves before and after each session, visualizing roots that connect them to the earth, allowing excess energy to release safely. For recipients, grounding exercises at the conclusion of each session provide a moment of calm and integration, giving the body and mind time to process the healing energies. Practitioners may guide recipients to visualize a gentle, protective shield surrounding them, creating a safe space for their energy to stabilize and absorb the benefits of the session.

Through these advanced practices, practitioners learn that energy healing is a process of co-creation between healer, recipient, and the Arcturian presence. Each healing session becomes an act of communion, a shared experience that transcends words and moves into the language of energy, resonance, and intention. The healing work resonates far beyond the physical, touching the deeper layers of the soul where true transformation can take place. This advanced level of energy healing nurtures a powerful alignment with the Arcturian frequency, empowering practitioners to serve as clear channels for healing and bringing the light of Arcturian wisdom into each session.

As practitioners further explore advanced Arcturian healing, they encounter multidimensional energies—subtle yet profound forces that extend beyond the physical and into realms where healing becomes a dialogue between spirit and energy.

The journey into multidimensional energy work begins with attunement. Practitioners enter a calm, receptive state, feeling their energy field expand and align with the Arcturian frequency. As they deepen this attunement, they become aware of the layered nature of energy, sensing currents that move within and beyond the physical realm. With each breath, they tune into these subtler frequencies, experiencing their presence as a quiet, expansive stillness that surrounds and fills them. This attunement allows practitioners to perceive and work with energies that are more refined than the physical, creating a channel that reaches across dimensions.

One advanced technique involves the use of "frequency layering"—an approach in which practitioners apply multiple frequencies within a single session, each resonating with a specific aspect of healing. For example, a lower frequency may be used to address physical imbalances, while a higher frequency works on the emotional or spiritual layers. Practitioners visualize these frequencies as layers of light, each a different hue or texture, carefully placing them within the recipient's energy field. This layering creates a comprehensive healing experience, allowing each frequency to address different dimensions simultaneously. Practitioners sense each layer settling into place, creating a resonance that permeates the recipient's entire being.

Another profound aspect of this work is energy anchoring. This technique involves anchoring specific frequencies into the recipient's energy field to support continued healing long after the session has concluded. Practitioners visualize these frequencies as symbols or geometric patterns, carefully chosen based on the recipient's needs, such as a pyramid for stability or a spiral for gentle release. These symbols are "anchored" by focusing intention and visualizing them as stable, enduring energies within the recipient's field. This anchoring effect creates a lasting resonance, allowing the healing process to continue subtly as the symbols hold the Arcturian frequency, encouraging gradual and deep transformation over time.

In working with complex healings, practitioners may also encounter blockages embedded in multiple layers of the energy body. The Arcturians guide practitioners to approach these blockages with patience and precision, using focused intention to dissolve or gently release them. Practitioners visualize the blockage as a dense or darkened area, directing a steady stream of light to gradually dissolve it. With each breath, they send compassionate, calming energy, observing as the blockage softens and clears. This method respects the recipient's pace, allowing each layer to release without force, creating a safe and gradual healing that integrates naturally.

To sustain focus in these multidimensional practices, practitioners employ breath sequences that deepen concentration and amplify the energy flow. One such technique is the "spiral breath," where practitioners visualize each inhale as a spiral of light that rises through the body, expanding awareness. With each exhale, they guide this spiral outward, directing energy precisely to areas in need. This breathing pattern enhances the healer's presence, ensuring that their energy remains grounded and focused throughout the session. Practitioners feel this spiral breath not only as a centering technique but as a way of attuning deeply to the energies at play, enabling them to work across dimensions with clarity.

In addition to breathing techniques, practitioners often work with Arcturian sound frequencies to amplify the effects of multidimensional healing. Specific tones or chants that resonate with high-frequency energies are incorporated, either through vocalization or sound instruments. These tones serve as bridges, opening gateways within the recipient's energy field and harmonizing with the frequencies of higher dimensions. Practitioners use sound in moments where they sense denser areas, allowing it to flow like a gentle wave, lifting and transforming blockages that reside in subtle, hidden layers. Each tone becomes a vibrational tool, a means of channeling healing energy that bypasses mental resistance and reaches the core of the issue.

After a session of multidimensional healing, grounding and integration become essential. Practitioners guide recipients through a gentle grounding visualization, envisioning roots extending from their feet into the earth, connecting them with the stability of the ground. Practitioners may also recommend simple activities to help recipients remain centered, such as touching a natural object or taking a quiet walk. This grounding helps stabilize the transformative energies accessed during the session, anchoring them within the body and mind to support a balanced integration.

As these advanced healing practices unfold, practitioners find that they are not merely performing techniques but engaging in a profound collaboration with Arcturian wisdom. Each session becomes a co-creative experience where the healer, recipient, and Arcturian energies interact seamlessly. Through these multidimensional practices, practitioners discover that healing is an expansive journey that transcends the physical and touches every aspect of being. They feel the presence of the Arcturians as guides and allies, empowering each healing session with compassion, insight, and the potential for profound transformation that ripples into every layer of existence.

Chapter 12
Energy Protection

As practitioners deepen their connection with Arcturian energies, they come to understand the importance of protecting their own energy field. Working with higher frequencies and connecting to others in healing and spiritual practices opens pathways that require care and attention to ensure balance. The journey into energy protection begins with awareness. Practitioners are encouraged to observe their own energy, becoming attuned to its shifts in response to different environments, people, and experiences. This attunement starts with a simple scanning practice: they close their eyes, take a few deep breaths, and direct their awareness to different areas of the body, sensing the energy present in each one. Through this observation, they begin to recognize subtle changes—whether sensations of warmth, heaviness, or calmness—helping them identify when their field feels either empowered or drained. This self-awareness serves as the foundation for protecting energy, enabling them to notice when they need to reinforce their boundaries.

Visualization becomes a key tool in energy protection, and one fundamental practice is the "shield of light." Practitioners envision a radiant, protective sphere surrounding their entire body, filling it with a light that reflects their personal intention for safety, calm, or clarity. This sphere acts as an energetic boundary, allowing positive, nourishing energies to enter while gently repelling any dense or disruptive forces. Practitioners are encouraged to customize this shield—perhaps visualizing it as a soft, permeable glow or as a stronger, mirrored surface depending on the need. This protective field is not rigid but adaptable, adjusting to each moment's intention, providing a sense of safety without creating resistance.

Grounding serves as another essential practice in maintaining energy protection. Through grounding, practitioners create a stabilizing connection with the earth, reinforcing their resilience. They visualize roots extending from their feet into the ground, drawing up earth energy that fills their body with a sense of strength and calm. This grounding practice connects them with the stabilizing energy of the earth, creating a balanced flow that prevents energetic depletion. By grounding before and after spiritual work, practitioners maintain a steady, centered field that supports energy protection in both ordinary and high-frequency experiences.

To enhance their energy protection, practitioners may work with specific Arcturian symbols and gestures that strengthen their aura. The Arcturians recommend symbols like the circle, triangle, or spiral, which carry unique vibrational qualities. Practitioners visualize these symbols surrounding or overlaying their energy field, infusing it with the symbol's protective essence. For example, a triangle placed at each point of the energy field can create a stabilizing structure, while a spiral may encourage gentle movement that disperses external energies without absorbing them. These symbols become energetic allies, enhancing the integrity of the aura and reinforcing the practitioner's connection to Arcturian wisdom.

Breathwork also plays an integral role in energy protection, particularly through cleansing breaths that help clear the field of any lingering energies. Practitioners begin with slow, deep inhales, drawing in pure, refreshing energy, and with each exhale, they release any tensions or energetic residues that do not belong to them. This breathwork not only cleanses but also revitalizes the energy field, restoring a natural state of clarity. As they practice, they feel the boundaries of their field becoming more defined, yet flexible, allowing them to interact with the world from a place of strength.

In addition to these practices, practitioners learn the importance of regular energy clearing, especially after engaging in healing or meditative work. Techniques such as "auric brushing" involve using the hands to gently sweep through their own energy field, moving from the head to the feet with the intention of clearing away any stagnant energies. With each motion, practitioners visualize unwanted energy dissolving and returning to the earth, transforming into light. This simple yet effective technique keeps the aura clear and free from external influences, allowing them to maintain their energetic vitality.

Practitioners are encouraged to develop a sense of energetic boundaries, an intuitive awareness of where their energy field ends and another's begins. Through practice, they cultivate a mental and spiritual "boundary" that defines their own space. This boundary, which does not isolate but respects each person's individuality, enables practitioners to engage fully while remaining energetically distinct. They approach interactions from a place of compassion and clarity, knowing that they can support others without merging or compromising their own field.

These practices of energy protection become a daily rhythm, a conscious nurturing of the energy field that supports every aspect of life and spiritual growth. As practitioners integrate these techniques, they sense a growing resilience and clarity within their field, experiencing each encounter from a place of inner peace. Through this foundation, they deepen their work with Arcturian energies, empowered to explore higher realms while staying grounded and protected, supported by the wisdom of the Arcturian presence.

With the foundational elements of energy protection established, practitioners move into deeper techniques for shielding, cleansing, and reinforcing their auric field. The Arcturians offer guidance on creating layers of protection that adapt to various energetic demands, from everyday interactions to intensive spiritual work. This advanced practice emphasizes proactive energy care, empowering practitioners to maintain a state of clarity and strength that nurtures both spiritual growth and well-being.

At the core of these practices is the concept of multi-layered protection. Practitioners are guided to visualize their energy field as having several layers, each with a distinct quality and purpose. The innermost layer, close to the physical body, is visualized as a gentle, nourishing light that sustains vitality and emotional balance. Surrounding this is a second layer that acts as a filter, allowing positive energies to flow freely while shielding from dense or discordant influences. Practitioners may imagine this layer as a soft glow or as a more structured form, like a lattice of light that adapts to their needs. The third layer forms the outermost boundary, offering a resilient shield that absorbs or deflects external energies. This multi-layered approach creates an adaptable field that responds naturally to different situations, allowing for a flexible yet firm boundary.

Another essential technique in advanced protection is the use of "mirror shielding." This method involves visualizing the outermost layer of the energy field as a mirror-like surface, one that reflects any negative energy or harmful intent back to its source, but without malice. Practitioners envision this reflective shield as calm and neutral, repelling only what is not in harmony with their field. By applying this mirror shielding, they create an energy boundary that maintains peace and safety, preventing their field from absorbing unwanted influences. This technique serves as a reminder of the Arcturian wisdom: protection is a state of neutrality and compassion, a boundary that safeguards without aggression.

In moments where heightened protection is needed, practitioners may engage in "light infusion," calling on Arcturian energies to fortify their shield. They visualize a powerful stream of light descending from above, filling and expanding each layer of their auric field with vibrant, purifying energy. As the light saturates their field, it intensifies their protection, creating an aura that feels radiant and impenetrable. This infusion process not only strengthens their defenses but also uplifts their entire energetic state, aligning them with the high frequencies of Arcturian guidance. Practitioners often find this practice especially helpful before entering environments or situations with heightened energetic activity.

Cleansing the energy of physical spaces becomes another focus in advanced protection, as the environments in which practitioners spend time can influence their own energy. The Arcturians recommend a technique known as "light sweeping" to clear spaces, which involves visualizing a wave of pure light moving through each room, dissolving any stagnant or discordant energy. Practitioners begin at one end of the space, envisioning this light sweeping through the area, touching every surface and corner until it feels renewed and clear. This technique establishes a harmonious environment that supports inner peace and energetic stability, creating a sanctuary where higher frequencies can flourish.

For further reinforcement, practitioners may incorporate crystals into their energy protection work. Crystals like black tourmaline, amethyst, or selenite are used as anchors, holding and amplifying protective intentions. Practitioners place these crystals in specific areas of their home, or even wear them, to create an ongoing field of protection. They cleanse these crystals regularly, using visualization or sound, ensuring that their energies remain clear and potent. The crystals become silent allies, enhancing the strength of the practitioner's aura and helping to maintain a consistent, protective field.

In moments of intense interaction, practitioners employ boundary-setting techniques that allow them to remain open yet energetically secure. Before entering such situations, they take a few breaths, visualizing a layer of light around their heart that maintains compassion but prevents the absorption of intense emotions or energies. This boundary-setting practice creates a balanced state where practitioners can engage fully without compromising their own energy field. After such encounters, they may perform a brief cleansing by brushing their hands around their body, visualizing any residual energy dispersing, restoring their field to its natural state.

After a day of work, interaction, or spiritual practice, practitioners conclude with a ritual of "energy closing." This involves a short, focused visualization where they envision their auric field retracting gently, becoming dense, stable, and calm. They sense each layer of protection closing softly, allowing their energy field to settle and integrate the experiences of the day. By closing their energy in this way, they reinforce a feeling of wholeness, grounding any residual energies and allowing their field to rest and recharge.

As these advanced practices of energy protection become part of their daily rhythm, practitioners find that their connection with Arcturian wisdom deepens. Their energy field feels more resilient, balanced, and clear, creating a solid foundation that supports both spiritual exploration and daily life. This journey in energy protection becomes a path of self-care, cultivating an environment where inner growth and outer stability coexist. Through these techniques, practitioners come to embody a state of peace and strength, a luminous presence that remains open to the world while firmly anchored in Arcturian light.

Chapter 13
Healing Crystals

The Arcturians teach that crystals, formed over eons within the earth, hold a wisdom and vibrational energy that resonates deeply with human consciousness. Each crystal carries a unique frequency, an energy signature that can amplify, balance, and transform the aura, aligning practitioners with the Arcturian presence and facilitating healing. Working with these stones becomes a practice of synergy, where natural earth energies merge with higher vibrations, creating a bridge between the physical and spiritual realms.

To begin, practitioners explore the basic properties of healing crystals, discovering how each type aligns with different aspects of their energy. Clear quartz, with its transparent clarity, amplifies intentions, strengthening any healing or spiritual work by increasing the resonance of one's thoughts and emotions. Rose quartz, in soft pink hues, nurtures the heart's energy, promoting love, compassion, and emotional healing. Amethyst, with its deep violet tone, calms the mind and opens the third eye, allowing for greater intuition and connection to higher realms. Practitioners take time to hold each stone, sensing the subtle vibrations it emits, and noticing how each interacts with their own energy field.

The practice of attuning to crystals involves more than observation; it is an active dialogue with their energies. Practitioners learn to cleanse each crystal before use, either by visualizing it immersed in purifying light or by placing it in natural elements such as sunlight, moonlight, or even saltwater. This cleansing clears any residual energies, resetting the crystal's vibration. With a cleansed stone, practitioners then set an intention, holding the crystal and visualizing their goal—whether it is clarity, healing, or protection—infusing the stone with their focused energy. This intentional process brings the crystal into alignment with their purpose, allowing its energies to work in harmony with their own.

One fundamental technique in crystal healing is the use of stones to balance and energize the chakras. Practitioners select crystals that resonate with each chakra, placing them on or near these energy centers to create alignment. Red stones, such as garnet or red jasper, are placed at the root chakra to ground and stabilize; orange stones like carnelian energize the sacral chakra, enhancing creativity and emotional flow; citrine, with its bright golden tone, activates the solar plexus, promoting confidence and personal power. Practitioners continue through each chakra, allowing the crystal's energy to flow, creating a balanced and harmonious field that facilitates healing.

Beyond individual chakra work, practitioners may create crystal grids, an arrangement of multiple stones that work together to amplify a specific intention. The Arcturians suggest that these grids serve as potent focal points, creating a stable and resonant energy field. Practitioners place the crystals in geometric patterns, each shape chosen to enhance their intention, such as a circle for unity, a triangle for focus, or a spiral for transformation. They visualize each crystal contributing its energy to the grid, forming a unified field that holds and magnifies their goal. Once created, practitioners may meditate near the grid, allowing its energy to align and support their own.

The Arcturians also teach practitioners how to use crystals for aura cleansing. After a day of work or interaction, practitioners can select a stone, such as selenite or black tourmaline, and gently pass it over their energy field, from head to feet. As the stone moves through the aura, practitioners visualize it absorbing or neutralizing any lingering energies that do not align with their own. This cleansing process restores clarity to the energy field, creating a refreshed and balanced state that supports ongoing spiritual growth. The act of cleansing with crystals becomes not only a practice of self-care but a reminder of the interconnectedness between human energy and the natural world.

Practitioners also learn to carry or wear crystals, keeping them close throughout the day as sources of steady support. They may wear amulets of protection, such as a pendant of labradorite or onyx, or carry small stones in a pocket or pouch. These crystals serve as subtle anchors, reinforcing their intentions and providing gentle energy throughout the day. Practitioners find that these personal stones become familiar allies, attuned to their unique vibration and offering support in moments of need or challenge.

Each interaction with crystals builds an intuitive understanding of their power, a language that goes beyond words and is felt through resonance and presence. Practitioners learn to sense which crystal is needed for each moment, drawn to a specific stone by intuition. The Arcturians encourage this trust in one's own guidance, knowing that each person's energy will naturally align with the stones that best serve their journey.

Through these practices, practitioners come to see crystals not merely as tools, but as partners in their spiritual evolution. These ancient beings of the earth hold frequencies that resonate with the Arcturian wisdom, offering energies that support, amplify, and guide. As practitioners work with these stones, they experience a grounding of the Arcturian light within the physical realm, bridging the earth and higher dimensions in a dance of energy that enriches every facet of their path.

In this advanced exploration of crystal work, practitioners deepen their relationship with these ancient beings, learning to harness their energies with more precision and intent. With guidance from the Arcturians, they discover techniques to amplify the vibrational properties of crystals, enhancing their alignment with higher frequencies and accessing energies that support healing, protection, and spiritual expansion.

One of the most profound techniques in this phase is the practice of "crystal attunement." Here, practitioners begin by quieting the mind, holding a crystal in hand, and breathing slowly, attuning their energy to the stone's subtle vibration. This attunement is a silent, receptive state, where the crystal's unique frequency begins to blend with the practitioner's energy. As the connection strengthens, practitioners sense their field harmonizing with the crystal, feeling a resonance that amplifies their intention. This attunement process aligns the crystal with the specific purpose it will serve, whether for healing, protection, or spiritual insight, creating a powerful energetic bond.

Once attuned, practitioners work with energizing techniques to amplify a crystal's frequency. One method involves visualizing a stream of light descending from above, flowing into the crystal. They focus on this light brightening the stone, filling it with high-vibrational energy that resonates with Arcturian frequencies. Some practitioners also incorporate breath, exhaling gently over the stone to infuse it with their own intention and life force. This infusion elevates the crystal's vibration, enabling it to act as a potent conductor of healing energy, ready to amplify any practice in which it is included.

Crystals also play a significant role in multidimensional healing, serving as anchors that stabilize and support the practitioner's journey across different levels of consciousness. Practitioners may select stones like amethyst, moldavite, or celestite, each known for its connection to higher realms and frequencies. When working with multidimensional energies, practitioners hold or place these stones near them, creating a steady energetic anchor that maintains alignment and protects the aura as they venture into higher vibrations. The crystal acts as a grounding force, harmonizing with the practitioner's energy and providing stability throughout the process.

The creation of a "crystal sanctuary" is another powerful technique introduced by the Arcturians. Practitioners arrange their chosen stones in a circle or geometric grid, a layout that holds specific vibrational qualities based on the stones used. This sacred space becomes a focal point for meditation, healing, or energy work, with each crystal contributing its unique frequency to create an environment rich in harmony and protection. Sitting within this sanctuary, practitioners feel enveloped in a field of pure, supportive energy, allowing them to access deeper states of awareness or amplify their healing work. The sanctuary serves as both a physical and energetic space, a meeting point for human intention and Arcturian light.

Practitioners also learn the art of crystal elixirs, a method for integrating crystal energy into physical form. They begin by selecting a crystal that is safe for water immersion, cleansing it, and placing it in a bowl of purified water. The water absorbs the crystal's vibration over several hours or under moonlight, creating an elixir that holds the essence of the stone. Once charged, practitioners can sip the elixir, bringing the crystal's frequency into their body, allowing its healing properties to resonate from within. This elixir method extends the reach of the crystal's energy, transforming it into a tangible experience that supports balance, clarity, or healing.

Cleansing and recharging crystals remain essential, especially after intensive work. Practitioners can cleanse stones by holding them under running water, visualizing any absorbed energies releasing, or by placing them in sunlight, moonlight, or near selenite, a crystal known for its self-cleansing properties. By regularly clearing their stones, practitioners ensure that each crystal maintains its pure, original frequency, ready to serve in new ways. The Arcturians remind practitioners that crystals, much like the human aura, benefit from regular energy care, reinforcing their ability to amplify healing with clarity and strength.

Practitioners incorporate crystals into their personal healing routines, placing specific stones on or around the body to address areas of need. When working with physical healing, they may place grounding stones like smoky quartz near the base of the spine, encouraging release and renewal. For emotional healing, rose quartz or rhodochrosite placed over the heart brings warmth and compassion, supporting the gentle release of old emotions. For spiritual insight, practitioners may place clear quartz or amethyst near the third eye, allowing the crystal to open pathways to higher wisdom. Each placement becomes a targeted infusion of energy, aligned with the Arcturian frequency and the practitioner's intent.

Through these refined techniques, practitioners experience crystals as more than tools; they become allies, silent yet profound, bridging the wisdom of the earth with the light of higher realms. Each interaction with these stones deepens the connection, amplifying the practitioner's own energy and aligning them more closely with the Arcturian guidance that illuminates their journey. Working with crystals in these advanced ways, practitioners find that their healing work transcends the physical, touching dimensions that resonate with both the earthly and the cosmic, integrating both into a single, harmonious path.

Chapter 14
Collective Rituals

The Arcturians emphasize the power of unity, guiding practitioners to engage in collective rituals that amplify healing, connection, and spiritual growth. These rituals, conducted with a group or community, create a synergy where individual energies blend into a cohesive force that supports each person's journey. When practitioners gather with a shared intent, their energies intertwine, generating a field of resonance that surpasses what any individual can achieve alone. The collective ritual becomes a sacred space, a moment where Arcturian presence merges with human energy, fostering deep transformation and unity.

To initiate a collective ritual, practitioners begin by setting a unified intention, an anchor that aligns everyone's energy toward a common purpose. This intention is simple yet potent, resonating with themes like healing, gratitude, or spiritual awakening. Each participant holds this shared vision, forming a mental and emotional alignment that strengthens the ritual's impact. Through this unity of purpose, the group creates a collective energy field, a harmonious resonance that amplifies their individual vibrations and invites the Arcturian presence.

One of the primary techniques in these collective rituals is the "Circle of Light." Participants gather in a circle, either physically or in spirit, creating a sacred geometry that enhances connection and openness. They visualize a stream of Arcturian light entering the space, flowing through each person, and linking their hearts with a radiant thread of energy. This thread weaves a network of light, forming a protective and nurturing boundary that surrounds the group. Each breath draws the participants deeper into this circle, each heartbeat resonating with the group's shared energy, fostering a bond that transcends the physical.

Within this circle, practitioners engage in guided visualization, a journey that connects them to higher realms. They collectively envision a scene of peace—a tranquil landscape, a starry sky, or a realm of pure light—allowing their minds to align with a state of calm and openness. As each person visualizes this shared space, it becomes tangible within the group's energy field, forming a sanctuary where they can encounter Arcturian wisdom and healing. In this collective visualization, each participant not only experiences their own journey but contributes to a unified vision that strengthens the entire group.

To deepen the ritual's resonance, sound and chant are often introduced. The group may use a single tone, like "Om" or a harmonious chant, to align their vibrations. This sound reverberates through the circle, blending each person's energy into a harmonious whole. The tone serves as a conduit, opening pathways within the group's energy field that welcome higher frequencies. Each voice joins, each vibration contributes, creating a resonance that extends beyond the group and touches realms of heightened awareness. The sound becomes an invitation to the Arcturian presence, inviting guidance and support into the ritual.

Practitioners may also incorporate movement, a flow that engages the body and spirit in harmony with the collective energy. Simple gestures, such as raising hands to the sky or placing them on the heart, synchronize the group's rhythm, blending physical action with spiritual intention. These movements serve as physical expressions of unity, a way for the group to feel connected not only through energy but through shared purpose. As each gesture is made, participants sense the energy flow within and around them, strengthening the collective field and deepening their connection to the ritual's intent.

In these rituals, each participant also holds a space of healing for the collective, offering their own energy as part of the group's transformation. As they sit in quiet focus, they visualize light radiating from their heart, joining the light from others in the circle. This unified light creates a sphere of healing energy that envelops the group, supporting each person's journey. Practitioners sense the gentle, encompassing warmth of this sphere, a reminder of the Arcturian compassion and wisdom that guides the collective ritual. Within this sphere, healing flows effortlessly, moving through each individual and returning to the group in a continuous, nurturing cycle.

At the ritual's conclusion, grounding practices bring each participant back to the present. Practitioners visualize roots extending from their feet, anchoring them into the earth, allowing any excess energy to dissipate gently. They sense the grounding as a steady, calm energy that supports integration, bringing clarity to the experiences shared in the ritual. As the group releases the collective field, they retain a part of its energy within them, a resonance that continues to support them individually even after the ritual has ended.

Through these collective rituals, practitioners experience a profound sense of unity, a shared spiritual journey that fosters both personal and communal growth. Each person's energy strengthens the group, while the group amplifies each individual's connection to the Arcturian wisdom. The collective ritual becomes a celebration of connection, a sacred act of creation where energies merge, guiding each participant toward healing, balance, and higher awareness. With each gathering, practitioners come to understand the power of unity, recognizing that the journey toward spiritual evolution is one shared, one that unfolds in harmony with the light of the Arcturians.

In this continuation of collective rituals, practitioners refine their understanding of group energy dynamics, developing advanced techniques for deepening spiritual connection within collective spaces. Under Arcturian guidance, these practices go beyond the individual to foster a unified field, amplifying both the energy and intention of each participant. As groups gather to engage in these rituals, they not only elevate their individual journeys but contribute to the collective vibration, creating a ripple effect of harmony and healing that extends beyond the ritual itself.

One advanced technique for deepening collective rituals is "harmonic resonance," where each participant attunes their energy field to a shared frequency. Practitioners begin by sitting in silence, allowing their breathing to slow and synchronize with the group's collective rhythm. This practice of harmonic resonance cultivates a single, cohesive energy, enabling each participant to feel part of a unified whole. As the group achieves this resonance, they sense a shared frequency within the space, a harmony that supports profound connections, inviting the presence of higher energies and making the ritual more impactful.

Another practice in advanced collective rituals is the use of guided group intention-setting. Before the ritual formally begins, each participant reflects on their personal intentions and then aligns them with a collective goal. Through quiet reflection or verbal expression, they state these intentions, infusing them with purpose and unity. This shared focus, held with mutual respect and alignment, establishes an energetic foundation for the ritual. As each participant aligns their intention with the group's purpose, a focused, directed energy field takes form, anchoring a harmonious space that is both individual and shared. This foundation amplifies the ritual's efficacy, fostering a deep sense of belonging and connection.

The use of light as a guiding force further enhances the ritual's depth. The Arcturians recommend a "pillar of light" technique, where participants envision a column of radiant, protective energy descending from above, flowing through the center of the circle and connecting each person. This pillar of light serves as a stabilizing force, grounding the group in the present moment and reinforcing their connection to the higher dimensions. As the light flows through the group, practitioners visualize it expanding, enveloping each person within a single, luminous field. The pillar becomes a beacon, holding the ritual's energy with clarity and strength, creating a direct link to Arcturian guidance.

Incorporating sound adds another layer of depth to these collective rituals. Practitioners may use harmonic chants, crystal bowls, or specific tones to elevate the energy within the space. Each sound resonates through the circle, blending individual vibrations into a single, cohesive frequency that carries the group's intention. As these sounds ripple outward, they refine and uplift the energy field, amplifying each participant's connection to both the group and higher realms. These harmonic frequencies open subtle gateways within the energy field, allowing Arcturian wisdom and healing energies to enter and support the ritual's purpose.

The practice of shared visualization becomes particularly potent in advanced collective rituals. Participants close their eyes and are guided through a visualization that aligns with the group's intention, such as envisioning a peaceful landscape or a place filled with light and unity. Each person visualizes the scene with as much clarity as possible, adding their unique vision to the collective field. This shared visualization creates a powerful mental and energetic framework, transforming individual thoughts into a unified vision that becomes tangible within the ritual space. In these moments, the group experiences a convergence of energy that transcends words, resonating deeply within each participant's heart.

Physical gestures can further anchor the ritual's energy. Participants may be guided to place a hand on the heart or extend palms outward, symbolizing both receptivity and unity. These gestures, synchronized with intention, create a shared rhythm that aligns each person's energy with the group's collective pulse. Movements, even subtle ones, become expressions of unity, grounding the group's energy and offering a physical reminder of their shared purpose. Each gesture embodies the collective spirit, transforming individual energy into a single, cohesive force that resonates within the circle.

In the final stage of the ritual, grounding and integration become essential. Practitioners are guided to visualize their energy field gently contracting, bringing the expansive energies experienced during the ritual back into their heart center. They imagine roots extending from their feet into the earth, grounding the shared energy within the present moment and allowing any excess to disperse safely. Through this grounding, the group's energy field stabilizes, anchoring the ritual's benefits within each participant and closing the space with clarity and peace.

As practitioners participate in these collective rituals, they experience a profound sense of interconnectedness, understanding that their spiritual journey is enriched through the presence of others. Each ritual becomes a bridge, connecting them not only to Arcturian guidance but to one another in mutual support and shared purpose. These advanced practices in collective ritual transform the group's energy into a living, evolving presence, where each person contributes to a resonance that carries beyond the circle, impacting the larger world with healing and light. Through each shared intention, each synchronized breath, and each visualization, the collective ritual becomes a powerful act of co-creation, guided by the light of the Arcturians and the unity of the group.

Chapter 15
Daily Integration

The journey with Arcturian energy becomes truly transformative when it is woven into the daily rhythm of life, creating a continuous flow that bridges spiritual practice and daily experience. Practitioners begin to sense the subtle yet profound impact of integrating Arcturian wisdom into ordinary moments, discovering that these energies can bring calm, balance, and alignment not only during meditation but in every interaction and activity. This integration process is about establishing a sustained connection that transforms each day into an expression of spiritual growth and inner harmony.

The first steps in this daily integration begin with setting an intention each morning, a moment where practitioners align their thoughts and energy with the Arcturian presence. Upon waking, they take a few quiet breaths, bringing their awareness to the heart and visualizing a soft, radiant light expanding from within. This light serves as both a protective and guiding force, filling the energy field with a sense of calm focus. Practitioners then set a simple intention, such as "I bring peace into my interactions" or "I remain centered in my true self." This intention becomes a gentle compass, guiding their thoughts and actions throughout the day, bringing Arcturian alignment into each moment.

Mindfulness practices support this integration, encouraging practitioners to maintain an awareness of their inner state as they go about daily activities. When engaging in tasks—whether working, cooking, or walking—they bring attention to their breath and body, grounding themselves in the present. This mindfulness helps them stay connected to their energy, noticing any shifts that occur due to external influences. When a challenging emotion or thought arises, practitioners pause, acknowledging it with calm and non-judgment, allowing it to flow through without attachment. This practice of presence transforms ordinary tasks into moments of grounding and clarity, where the Arcturian energy flows unobstructed, creating a sense of inner peace.

Grounding techniques become essential in maintaining this state of integration. Practitioners periodically visualize roots extending from their feet, anchoring them to the earth. They sense this grounding energy as a steady pulse, a connection that strengthens their resilience and balances their energy field. This grounding practice is especially helpful during moments of stress or fatigue, providing a stabilizing force that brings them back to a centered, balanced state. Each time they ground, they reinforce a connection to both the physical and spiritual realms, creating a harmonious flow that supports their alignment with Arcturian guidance.

Another key practice in daily integration is conscious breathing, a tool for aligning the body, mind, and spirit with each inhale and exhale. Practitioners periodically take slow, deep breaths, visualizing each inhale as a wave of light that flows through the body, filling every cell with calm and clarity. Each exhale releases any tension, negative thoughts, or energies that do not align with their intention. This breathing practice serves as a reset, clearing the mind and refining the energy field. By tuning into their breath, practitioners feel a direct connection to the Arcturian presence, a quiet reminder of their inner light and the calmness it brings to each moment.

For practitioners, each interaction becomes an opportunity to express the principles and energies they cultivate in their spiritual practices. They bring compassion, patience, and active listening into conversations, viewing each exchange as a chance to embody the Arcturian presence. When conflict arises, they practice calm detachment, observing their reactions without being swept away by them. By maintaining this centeredness, they contribute to the harmony of their environment, radiating a peaceful presence that often diffuses tension. In each interaction, practitioners see the influence of Arcturian guidance, recognizing the subtle ways in which their own inner balance can positively impact those around them.

Practitioners are also encouraged to use brief visualization practices throughout the day to realign their energy. During breaks or moments of rest, they may close their eyes and envision themselves bathed in a sphere of Arcturian light, feeling it cleanse and replenish their field. This light fills their energy centers, restoring balance and vibrancy, dissolving any discordant energies they may have encountered. These short visualizations serve as moments of recalibration, allowing practitioners to maintain a high vibrational state even amid daily demands.

As they bring these practices into each day, practitioners begin to notice a subtle but steady transformation. Their energy field feels clearer, their responses more grounded, and their mind more attuned to higher awareness. They feel less reactive, more observant, and better able to maintain a perspective rooted in compassion and understanding. These shifts reflect the gradual integration of Arcturian energy into their being, a quiet alignment that becomes visible through the calm, balanced way they navigate life's challenges and experiences.

As night approaches, practitioners complete their day with a closing practice, reviewing the experiences, emotions, and insights gained. They take a few moments in reflection, sensing any areas of gratitude or areas where they wish to grow. Through this reflection, they create a space for self-compassion, embracing each experience as part of their journey, and releasing anything that does not serve their growth. They may visualize any residual energy flowing into the earth or returning to the Arcturian light, completing the day with a sense of peace and readiness for rest.

Through these simple, steady practices, practitioners discover that integrating Arcturian wisdom is not about changing their lives overnight but about embracing each moment as an opportunity for connection and growth. With each breath, each thought, each interaction, they feel a deepening resonance with the Arcturian presence, a guiding light that shapes their journey into one of continuous learning, balance, and peace. Their lives become a reflection of the spiritual work they cultivate, bridging the sacred and the everyday into a single, harmonious path.

In this advanced exploration of daily integration, practitioners delve into practices that foster a seamless flow between Arcturian guidance and everyday life. Building on initial techniques, they now explore methods to strengthen the vibrational connection to higher frequencies, adapting these energies to the unique rhythm and demands of daily experiences. Practitioners learn to embody Arcturian light not only in moments of stillness but through continuous awareness and energy maintenance, enriching their personal growth and creating a life anchored in spiritual alignment.

A primary focus in advanced integration is the use of energy maintenance practices that sustain a steady frequency throughout the day. Practitioners cultivate a gentle, ongoing awareness of their energetic state, sensing shifts as they move through different environments and encounters. This awareness begins with the simple act of "energy scanning," a technique where they pause momentarily, breathe deeply, and observe any sensations or emotions in the body. With practice, this scanning becomes second nature, allowing them to detect when their energy has been affected by an external source or internal reaction. This sensitivity enables them to address minor imbalances before they accumulate, creating a consistently aligned state.

One method for realigning energy during the day is the "inner flame" technique, in which practitioners visualize a small, steady flame within the heart or solar plexus. This flame represents their core essence, a point of constant, calm light that remains unaffected by outer influences. When they feel their energy disperse or weaken, they bring attention back to this flame, visualizing it growing brighter and more radiant. This simple visualization serves as a grounding anchor, helping practitioners reconnect with their inner strength and restore balance.

Another advanced practice is adapting Arcturian techniques to specific daily challenges. For example, in moments of stress or high energy demands, practitioners visualize an "energy bubble," a translucent sphere surrounding their body, filled with soothing blue or violet light. This bubble acts as a buffer, preserving their personal energy and preventing external forces from affecting their equilibrium. Practitioners can renew this energy bubble throughout the day as needed, adjusting its strength and qualities based on the environment, thereby creating a flexible boundary that maintains alignment.

Incorporating mantra and affirmation work brings a continuous thread of Arcturian energy into daily life. Practitioners select specific words or phrases that resonate with their personal goals, such as "I embody peace" or "I am grounded in truth." These affirmations are repeated quietly or in the mind throughout the day, especially in moments of transition or challenge. The Arcturians emphasize that these words, when spoken with intent, reinforce the mind's alignment with higher frequencies, creating subtle but profound shifts in thought and energy. Through these affirmations, practitioners maintain a clear, focused presence that uplifts and aligns them in each moment.

Arcturian breathing techniques, which enhance the flow of energy through the body, become vital tools in this advanced integration. One effective practice is the "three-part breath," where practitioners inhale into the lower lungs, then the middle, and finally the upper chest, exhaling in reverse. Each breath cycle gently clears and harmonizes the chakras, aligning the physical and spiritual bodies. This rhythm becomes a tool for centering the mind and body, a way of returning to balance even in demanding moments. With practice, this breathing becomes a natural response to tension, grounding practitioners instantly and enabling them to face challenges with clarity.

To deepen their daily connection, practitioners incorporate "sacred pauses," moments where they stop briefly to connect with the Arcturian energy in the midst of activity. This pause can be as simple as a deep breath, a silent affirmation, or a moment of visualizing a sphere of light around them. Practitioners sense this moment as a reconnection with their higher self, a quiet realignment with the Arcturian guidance. These sacred pauses, integrated regularly, transform their day into a series of intentional moments, bridging the spiritual and the physical.

Reflection at the day's end offers practitioners a way to integrate insights and refine their practices. In a few moments of quiet review, they consider the day's experiences, noting times when they felt aligned and moments when their energy wavered. Rather than judging, they observe with curiosity, gaining awareness of patterns and areas that need support. Through this reflection, they come to see each day as a lesson, a process of refining their ability to stay connected to Arcturian guidance. This quiet contemplation grounds them, releasing any remaining energies from the day and inviting balance and peace into the mind.

Advanced integration also includes expressing Arcturian qualities within relationships and communication. Practitioners focus on qualities such as empathy, active listening, and calm engagement, observing how these energies transform their interactions. In conversations, they practice heart-centered awareness, listening fully and speaking with intention. When faced with tension, they envision a sphere of light between themselves and others, allowing for open connection while preserving their energy field. This practice not only enhances communication but also infuses the space with Arcturian harmony, creating interactions that are uplifting for all involved.

As practitioners bring these advanced techniques into their daily lives, they begin to sense a transformation in how they move through the world. They feel attuned to their energy field, noticing subtle shifts that once went unrecognized. Emotions and thoughts become easier to observe without attachment, leading to a calm clarity that fosters growth and insight. Each moment becomes an opportunity to embody Arcturian presence, to create harmony within and share it with the world around them.

Through these daily integration practices, practitioners establish a life where spiritual alignment and daily action coexist seamlessly. The journey with Arcturian guidance becomes a living, breathing reality—each day an opportunity for connection, growth, and expansion. Practitioners experience life as an expression of their highest self, walking a path where every moment reflects the peace, balance, and insight fostered through their spiritual journey.

Chapter 16
Spiritual Awakening

The path of spiritual awakening begins with a quiet stirring, a sense that there is more to existence than meets the eye. For those on the Arcturian journey, this awakening is guided by energies that encourage a deeper understanding of the self, illuminating the inner realms and fostering a connection with higher consciousness. The Arcturians, with their compassionate presence, offer practices that help practitioners to tap into this latent potential, opening the door to a profound and transformative journey within.

The initial steps in awakening focus on self-awareness, a process that encourages practitioners to observe their thoughts, feelings, and actions with clarity. Practitioners start by cultivating a gentle, non-judgmental awareness, noticing their inner world as they would observe a landscape. This mindful observation reveals patterns—thoughts that repeat, emotions that linger, reactions that arise. Through this practice, practitioners begin to see the layers that compose their identity, understanding the beliefs and experiences that shape their perceptions. This self-awareness is not about critique but about understanding, a foundation that reveals both strengths and areas for growth.

Guided reflection becomes a central technique in this awakening process, offering practitioners a way to connect with their deeper desires and purpose. The Arcturians encourage practitioners to set aside time for contemplative reflection, asking open-ended questions such as, "What are my true aspirations?" or "What energies do I wish to cultivate in my life?" With each question, practitioners listen attentively to their inner responses, sensing the deeper desires that may have remained unspoken. This reflection connects them to a part of themselves that transcends daily roles and responsibilities, fostering a connection with the true self that lies beneath.

Meditative practices hold a special place in awakening, as they provide a space for direct experience of inner stillness and expanded awareness. Practitioners are guided to enter meditation with a focus on calm breathing and relaxation, letting go of external distractions and turning inward. With each breath, they envision a light in the heart center, soft and radiant, growing brighter with each inhalation. This light represents their true essence, a point of clarity and peace that connects them to higher realms. As they sit in this light, they sense a quiet expansion, a feeling of openness that transcends the boundaries of the physical self. In these moments of meditation, practitioners experience a glimpse of the vastness within, a doorway to the consciousness that connects them with all of existence.

A key element in awakening is the release of attachments—patterns, thoughts, and emotions that no longer serve one's growth. The Arcturians offer gentle techniques for identifying and releasing these attachments, helping practitioners to free themselves from old limitations. Practitioners begin by bringing to mind any lingering thoughts or feelings that feel heavy or restrictive, observing them without attachment. Through visualization, they imagine these attachments as wisps of smoke, gently dissipating as they exhale. This process of release lightens the energy field, creating space for new experiences and insights to flow in. Each release feels like shedding an old layer, a return to one's natural state of balance and openness.

Practitioners are also encouraged to explore the concept of acceptance as a pathway to awakening. This acceptance is not passive but an active embrace of the present moment, recognizing each experience as part of a greater journey. Practitioners observe themselves, their circumstances, and even their challenges with a sense of compassion, understanding that each holds a lesson. By embracing acceptance, they release resistance and allow their energy to flow freely, creating an open channel through which higher guidance can enter. Acceptance becomes a powerful ally in the journey of awakening, a doorway to inner peace that transforms even difficult experiences into opportunities for growth.

Dreamwork is another practice that enriches awakening, as the Arcturians believe dreams offer insights from the subconscious and higher realms. Practitioners are encouraged to keep a journal by their bedside, noting any dreams upon waking. With time, they begin to notice patterns, symbols, and messages that reflect their inner journey. Dreams become a language of the soul, offering guidance, affirmations, and even glimpses of potential futures. Practitioners find that their dreams often align with their waking intentions, reinforcing the insights gained in meditation and reflection.

Energy alignment supports this journey, as practitioners work with Arcturian light to harmonize the chakras and clear the aura. Simple techniques, such as visualizing a stream of light moving through each chakra, create a balanced flow of energy that supports clarity and intuition. This alignment opens pathways to spiritual perception, allowing practitioners to sense subtle shifts in energy and guiding them toward elevated states of awareness. Each alignment practice serves as a reminder of their inner light, grounding them in their true essence while expanding their consciousness.

Throughout this journey, practitioners feel a growing connection with the Arcturian presence, a quiet yet profound companionship that supports their awakening. The Arcturians, as guides, offer subtle encouragement and gentle guidance, helping practitioners trust their inner wisdom. This connection brings reassurance during moments of uncertainty, a reminder that they are not alone in this journey. The Arcturian presence fosters a sense of belonging and support, creating a safe and nurturing environment where practitioners can explore their consciousness without fear.

As practitioners continue these practices, they begin to experience a shift in perception. The world appears more vibrant, thoughts become clearer, and emotions feel balanced. They see beyond the surface of everyday life, sensing the interconnectedness of all things. This awakening is not a destination but a process, a gradual unfolding of awareness that brings them closer to their true self with each step. The journey with the Arcturians becomes an exploration of inner realms, a path where each moment reveals a new depth, a new insight, and a profound sense of harmony with the universe.

As practitioners delve deeper into the journey of spiritual awakening, they encounter an even richer experience of self-discovery and expansion. This phase of awakening is about refining perception, expanding consciousness, and cultivating a profound sense of interconnectedness. With guidance from the Arcturians, practitioners are led through practices that reveal subtler dimensions of awareness, helping them embrace a more holistic view of their true essence and their role within the vast tapestry of existence.

Central to this stage is the practice of self-evaluation, where practitioners move beyond basic self-awareness into a deeper exploration of their core beliefs, intentions, and motivations. In a quiet space, they are encouraged to reflect on questions that reach into the heart of their being: "What aspects of myself am I ready to embrace or release?" or "How do I embody compassion, clarity, and love?" Through this introspection, practitioners begin to see the patterns that shape their lives, gaining insight into aspects of their personality, relationships, and life choices. This deeper self-evaluation offers clarity and empowers them to align their actions with their spiritual aspirations, embracing an authentic path of self-expression.

Purification practices take on greater importance as practitioners release residual energies and patterns that may hinder their growth. The Arcturians guide them to visualize purifying light flowing through the body, dissolving any remaining attachments, fears, or doubts. Practitioners may envision this light as a gentle wave that moves through each cell, carrying away any energies that no longer serve them. As this light flows, they feel a sense of renewal, a lightening of the energy field that creates space for higher vibrations. Through this purification, they experience an inner clarity, a sense of being cleansed and aligned with their true essence.

Acceptance and release become transformative allies in this phase. The Arcturians encourage practitioners to approach this journey with self-compassion, allowing all emotions and experiences to arise without resistance. Acceptance means embracing every part of the self—both strengths and vulnerabilities—with understanding. Practitioners are guided to observe difficult emotions, memories, or beliefs without attachment, allowing each to be seen and released naturally. With each act of release, they feel a gentle expansion within, sensing a newfound spaciousness that welcomes growth and transformation. This process of acceptance and release strengthens their inner resilience, creating a solid foundation from which to explore higher realms of consciousness.

As practitioners continue, they learn to open to new perceptions, developing an expanded awareness that reaches beyond physical senses. The Arcturians guide them through exercises in intuitive awareness, where practitioners tune into subtle impressions or energies in their surroundings. Through quiet focus, they begin to sense layers of reality—energies, emotions, and vibrations that are part of the unseen world. This heightened perception fosters a greater understanding of their connection to all living beings, an awareness that transcends individuality and invites them to experience life as part of a unified whole. With practice, practitioners cultivate a natural attunement to these subtle dimensions, experiencing a deepened relationship with the world around them.

Meditative states become a doorway to the boundless aspects of consciousness. In moments of stillness, practitioners allow their awareness to expand, visualizing themselves surrounded by Arcturian light that elevates their consciousness.

They let go of any need to control the experience, simply resting in the quiet presence that arises. In these elevated states, they often encounter insights or moments of profound clarity—visions, symbols, or impressions that resonate with their inner journey. Practitioners are encouraged to stay open to whatever arises, trusting that each experience is part of their awakening. These meditative states offer glimpses into higher realms, allowing practitioners to feel the presence of the Arcturians as guides and allies on this expansive journey.

An important technique in this phase is energy alignment with planetary consciousness, where practitioners connect their awakening to the collective growth of humanity and Earth. Through meditation, they visualize themselves as channels of light, grounding Arcturian energy into the earth, envisioning this light spreading across landscapes, people, and ecosystems. This practice not only strengthens their personal awakening but supports the collective evolution of consciousness. Practitioners experience a sense of purpose, realizing that their personal journey is intertwined with the greater whole, and that each act of self-growth contributes to a brighter, more harmonious world.

As this connection to planetary consciousness deepens, practitioners are guided to anchor their experiences through journaling. In this practice, they capture insights, reflections, and impressions from meditation or daily interactions. Writing becomes a sacred space, a mirror reflecting their inner journey and helping them integrate each experience into conscious understanding. The journal holds the evolution of their thoughts and awareness, capturing moments of growth, transformation, and clarity. Through this continuous self-reflection, practitioners observe their awakening unfold as a living journey, an evolving process that deepens with each insight.

Practitioners also learn techniques for grounding high-vibrational experiences, allowing them to integrate these elevated states into their daily lives with ease. After each meditative or intuitive practice, they are encouraged to visualize roots connecting them to the earth, bringing any remaining energy down through the body and anchoring it into the ground. This grounding practice ensures that insights from higher states remain accessible, enriching their life and actions in the physical world. Through this grounding, practitioners learn to bridge the realms of spirit and matter, making each awakening experience a tangible part of their daily path.

With each of these practices, practitioners feel themselves moving closer to the Arcturian presence, sensing their guidance not as something external but as a resonance that arises from within. This presence becomes a subtle but constant companion, a reminder of their interconnectedness with the universe and the inner light that guides them. In each moment of clarity, they experience awakening as a deep, inner knowing, a recognition that the truth they seek is already within them.

The journey of awakening becomes a path where every thought, emotion, and interaction carries potential for insight. Each step reveals a greater depth of self-understanding, each moment of stillness an opportunity to touch higher consciousness. Practitioners find that their lives are no longer a series of separate events but a continuous flow of awareness, a harmonious dance between self and universe. Through the wisdom of the Arcturians, the journey of awakening unfolds as a return to the essence of being, a discovery of the boundless spirit that lies at the heart of all life.

Chapter 17
Arcturian Intuition

Intuition acts as a bridge between the known and the unknown, connecting practitioners to the subtle guidance of the Arcturian presence. As practitioners develop and strengthen their intuition, they begin to perceive subtle energies and messages that go beyond ordinary understanding.

The journey into intuition begins with the practice of inner stillness, a state of receptivity where the mind settles and becomes open to subtle impressions. Practitioners are guided to find a quiet space, close their eyes, and breathe gently, allowing any thoughts or distractions to fade. This stillness serves as a gateway to the intuitive mind, creating a space where Arcturian guidance can gently flow in. In this calm, practitioners begin to sense a quiet inner voice, distinct from their own thoughts, a voice that offers gentle nudges or impressions. Through daily practice, they learn to recognize this voice, distinguishing it from ordinary thought patterns.

A key element of developing intuition is the practice of focused attention. Practitioners choose a small object—perhaps a stone, flower, or candle flame—and observe it with full awareness, noting every detail without distraction. This practice sharpens their ability to focus, training the mind to remain attentive and receptive. The Arcturians suggest that this focus acts as a stepping stone to intuitive perception, enabling practitioners to observe subtle shifts in energy and feeling. By honing this attentiveness, practitioners cultivate an awareness that allows them to notice intuitive insights as they arise, even in the midst of daily life.

To deepen intuition, practitioners are introduced to a practice of "inner listening." In a quiet meditative state, they bring their attention to the heart center, breathing gently and asking an open-ended question, such as "What guidance is there for me today?" They then sit in silence, noticing any impressions, words, or images that emerge without forcing an answer. This inner listening opens a pathway to Arcturian wisdom, allowing practitioners to receive insights that may come as feelings, symbolic images, or thoughts that hold a unique resonance. With practice, they develop trust in this guidance, learning to interpret the subtle language of their inner self.

The Arcturians also encourage practitioners to explore intuitive writing, a technique where thoughts flow freely onto paper without judgment or editing. Sitting with a pen and journal, practitioners ask a question or set an intention, and then write continuously, allowing whatever arises to flow onto the page. This stream-of-consciousness writing taps into the intuitive mind, often bringing forth insights that surprise or inspire. Through this process, practitioners learn to bypass the analytical mind, allowing deeper truths and guidance to surface. The journal becomes a companion on the intuitive journey, capturing insights and serving as a record of the evolving connection with Arcturian wisdom.

Dream recall and interpretation further support the awakening of intuition. Practitioners are encouraged to keep a dream journal, noting their dreams immediately upon waking. With time, they begin to notice recurring themes, symbols, or messages that offer guidance. The Arcturians view dreams as a portal to higher dimensions, where the subconscious can communicate directly with spiritual realms. Practitioners gradually develop an intuitive sense of their dreams' meanings, learning to distinguish between literal interpretations and symbolic messages. This practice helps them understand the language of their subconscious and opens a path to more direct forms of Arcturian communication.

An essential aspect of intuitive development is the cultivation of trust. Practitioners are guided to honor the insights they receive, even if they seem subtle or uncertain. They start by following these intuitions in small, safe ways, such as choosing a route, making simple decisions, or reaching out to someone they felt guided to connect with. Each time they follow an intuitive nudge, they reinforce the connection to their inner guidance. As they build this trust, they become more comfortable relying on intuition in larger areas of life, sensing the flow of Arcturian support and understanding that each insight is part of a greater alignment.

Another foundational practice involves visualizing a "field of light" surrounding them, enhancing their receptivity to Arcturian guidance. In a calm state, practitioners imagine themselves encased in a gentle, luminous sphere, feeling it amplify their sensitivity to subtle energies. They may even invite Arcturian light into this field, feeling it elevate their frequency and clear their awareness. This visualization creates a receptive space, a protected environment where they can attune to intuition without interference, building a stronger and clearer channel for guidance to flow through.

Through these practices, practitioners begin to see intuition as a natural aspect of their being, a sense that connects them with both their inner wisdom and the Arcturian presence. The insights they receive are no longer seen as random impressions but as meaningful guidance that supports their spiritual journey. As they develop their intuitive abilities, they feel a deeper connection to the Arcturian energy, sensing a quiet companionship that offers gentle support and inspiration.

Practitioners are encouraged to bring intuition into everyday life, recognizing that each moment offers opportunities to listen, observe, and trust. The more they honor their intuitive insights, the stronger their connection to Arcturian guidance becomes, transforming each experience into a step on the path of spiritual alignment and inner knowing. In this process, intuition becomes more than a skill—it evolves into a bridge that continuously connects them with the realms of wisdom and light, guiding them through life with clarity, trust, and peace.

As practitioners deepen their journey into intuition, they engage with advanced practices that refine their perception and sensitivity to Arcturian guidance. These techniques allow them to tap into higher levels of awareness, distinguishing between intuitive insights and personal thoughts, and interpreting the subtle messages that arise from their inner connection with the Arcturians. This phase of intuitive development builds on earlier practices, expanding into realms where the practitioner becomes a more precise and receptive vessel for higher wisdom.

A central aspect of this deeper intuitive work is the cultivation of clarity. Practitioners are guided to maintain a steady practice of mental and emotional cleansing, using breathwork and visualization to create an open and receptive state. They begin each session by breathing slowly, envisioning a radiant light filling their mind, clearing away any lingering thoughts or distractions. This purification process strengthens the clarity of the intuitive channel, allowing the practitioner to sense impressions with greater sharpness. Over time, they notice that these practices not only prepare the mind for insight but also build a lasting state of clarity that flows into daily life.

In this advanced phase, practitioners are introduced to the technique of "multi-sensory perception," a practice that expands intuitive awareness beyond the usual five senses. With guidance, they learn to notice subtle sensations, such as shifts in energy or slight tingling in the body, which indicate the presence of Arcturian communication. For example, practitioners might feel warmth when receiving positive affirmation or a sense of calm when alignment is present. These sensations, though subtle, act as signals, helping practitioners differentiate intuitive insights from everyday thoughts. By learning to tune into these sensory cues, they create a direct and reliable connection with the Arcturian realm, where every sensation becomes part of a larger, intuitive language.

Advanced intuition also involves the ability to interpret symbolic messages, as Arcturian guidance often presents itself through imagery, colors, or archetypal symbols. Practitioners enter a meditative state and allow images to naturally arise in the mind's eye, observing these visions without judgment. As symbols appear, they gently explore their meanings, trusting the associations that come to mind. For instance, the image of a flowing river might suggest emotional release, while a rising sun could indicate new beginnings. Practitioners find that these symbols communicate nuanced guidance, resonating with their current state or path. Through this symbolic language, they receive messages that bypass the analytical mind, offering insights that speak directly to the soul.

Practitioners are also encouraged to refine their skills in "Arcturian clairvoyance," where they learn to access intuitive insights beyond the limitations of time and space. In a meditative state, they practice envisioning a question or area of focus, allowing images or impressions to emerge that provide clarity. This practice can reveal potential outcomes, opportunities, or unseen influences, offering a broader view of circumstances. The Arcturians emphasize that this ability is not about predicting rigid outcomes but about sensing the energies that surround a situation, allowing practitioners to navigate life with greater wisdom. By developing this clairvoyance, practitioners attune themselves to a timeless space, where insight flows freely and reveals pathways aligned with their higher purpose.

In order to ground these intuitive experiences, practitioners are introduced to a journaling technique known as "intuitive synthesis." After a session, they write down the symbols, images, or impressions they received, and then take a few moments to explore their meanings. This process helps them interpret and integrate intuitive messages into everyday understanding. Practitioners find that patterns often emerge across entries, revealing deeper truths and guidance that may not be immediately apparent. By engaging in this reflective writing, they anchor the intuitive experience in a tangible form, making it easier to apply insights to practical decisions and personal growth.

Practitioners are also encouraged to perform daily "energy alignment" practices to keep their intuitive channels clear and stable. These practices involve visualizing a column of light extending from above, flowing through each chakra and grounding into the earth. This light brings balance to the energetic centers, ensuring that intuition is not influenced by emotional or mental imbalances. With each alignment, practitioners feel a renewed connection to their inner calm, a state that supports clear and steady intuition. Over time, these energy practices create a stable foundation, where intuitive impressions can flow without obstruction or distortion.

To deepen intuitive trust, practitioners are taught to engage with "silent witnessing," an exercise in observing thoughts, emotions, and intuitive impressions without judgment or attachment. In moments of quiet, they simply witness what arises within, allowing thoughts and sensations to flow naturally. Through this witnessing, practitioners develop a neutral space within the mind, one where intuition can arise freely and clearly. This neutrality is a powerful ally in intuitive work, helping practitioners to discern true guidance from personal desires or fears. With practice, silent witnessing becomes a state they carry into daily life, creating a continuous openness to Arcturian insight.

Practitioners are introduced to the concept of "intuitive coherence," a state where inner guidance aligns seamlessly with action. They learn to recognize when an intuition feels deeply right—a resonance in the heart and mind that brings a sense of peace. This coherence signals that the intuition is aligned with their highest path. Practitioners are encouraged to act upon these coherent intuitions, trusting that each step taken in alignment with inner guidance brings them closer to spiritual harmony. In this way, intuition becomes not just a tool for insight but a compass that guides daily actions and choices with clarity and purpose.

Through these practices, practitioners come to understand intuition as an intrinsic aspect of their being, a channel through which the Arcturian light flows. They feel an intimate connection to the Arcturian presence, a constant support that speaks in symbols, sensations, and impressions. Each intuitive experience becomes a reminder of their spiritual journey, a reflection of the inner wisdom that lies within.

As practitioners refine these abilities, they find that intuition transforms their experience of life. Choices feel guided, relationships deepen with understanding, and moments of stillness bring rich, subtle insights. The boundary between the physical and the spiritual becomes fluid, with intuition acting as a bridge that reveals the wisdom present in each moment. Through this advanced practice, intuition is not merely heightened but becomes woven into the fabric of their being, a silent guidance that brings peace, insight, and unity with the Arcturian path.

Chapter 18
Group Practices

As practitioners deepen their journey with Arcturian energy, they discover the transformative potential of shared spiritual practice. Group work amplifies healing and expansion, creating a unique field of energy that enhances individual and collective growth. The Arcturians emphasize that when individuals gather with shared intent, the combined energy exceeds the sum of each person's contribution, generating a resonance that opens pathways to higher realms and deeper insights. In these group settings, practitioners not only advance their personal growth but contribute to a collective vibration that radiates healing and harmony outward.

Forming a group dedicated to Arcturian practices begins with intention setting. Practitioners gather with a shared purpose, establishing a common goal that aligns with the Arcturian principles of healing, compassion, and consciousness expansion. Whether the intent is meditation, healing work, or energy alignment, this collective focus becomes the foundation for each session. Practitioners take a moment to tune into this shared intention, visualizing it as a light that connects each person within the circle. As the group aligns with this purpose, they create a unified energy field that strengthens their connection to one another and to the Arcturian presence.

An essential technique in group practice is synchronized breathing, where each participant breathes in rhythm with the group. This simple yet profound practice harmonizes the group's energy field, bringing coherence to their shared focus.

Practitioners close their eyes, inhale deeply together, and then exhale in unison, feeling their individual energies blending into a single pulse. With each synchronized breath, the group experiences a sense of unity that transcends individuality, a state that opens them to higher frequencies and aligns them with the collective intention. This breathing practice acts as a grounding force, creating a steady rhythm that stabilizes the energy of the group.

Visualization plays a pivotal role in group practices, guiding practitioners to hold a shared image or intention. One effective visualization is the creation of a "circle of light," where each participant imagines a radiant sphere of energy forming around the group. This sphere acts as both a protective boundary and a source of elevated energy, connecting each person within a field of harmony and alignment. Practitioners sense the light growing brighter with each moment, feeling it cleanse and elevate the group's vibration. This circle of light also serves as an invitation for Arcturian energies, creating a sacred space where higher guidance and healing can flow freely.

In group meditation, practitioners are encouraged to focus on a shared vision or goal, such as global healing, personal transformation, or enhanced intuition. As each participant holds this vision in mind, they contribute to a powerful collective thought-form that gains strength from the group's unified focus. Practitioners may feel the presence of Arcturian energy as a gentle warmth or calm that fills the space, supporting their intentions. This meditative focus becomes a channel for higher energies, drawing on the group's combined strength to amplify the intention and send it outward, creating ripples of healing and alignment beyond the circle.

Another key element of group practice is energy exchange, where practitioners support one another through focused intention and compassionate presence. Practitioners pair up or form small groups, each taking turns as the giver and receiver of energy. In this exchange, one person relaxes into a receptive state while the others visualize healing energy flowing into them. The Arcturians encourage practitioners to focus on unconditional support, allowing the energy to flow naturally without force. This practice of giving and receiving creates a balanced flow of energy that nourishes each person, reinforcing the group's bond and enhancing individual healing.

Sound and chanting further elevate the energy within group practice. The group may begin with a unified sound, such as "Om" or a specific tone, which they repeat together in harmony. This sound acts as a resonance, vibrating through each person and connecting their energies on a subtle level. Practitioners feel the sound resonating within, aligning their energy fields with one another and creating a powerful collective vibration. This harmonic chanting also creates an atmosphere of sacredness, inviting Arcturian energies to support and guide the group's practice. As the sound fades, practitioners remain in silence, sensing the elevated energy field that now surrounds them.

Group practices are further enhanced through guided exercises in energy alignment. Practitioners may begin by grounding their energies individually, visualizing roots extending from their feet into the earth, creating stability within the shared space. Following this grounding, the group collectively visualizes a column of Arcturian light descending from above, connecting each person and anchoring into the center of their gathering. This column serves as a conduit for higher energies, allowing each person to draw on Arcturian light for personal balance and collective harmony. The shared alignment practice strengthens the group's energy field, creating a stable foundation for the deeper work that follows.

At the conclusion of each session, practitioners engage in a closing ritual to integrate and ground the energies they have shared. They may hold hands or place a hand over the heart, taking a moment of silence to express gratitude for the collective experience. This closing ritual brings a sense of completion, allowing each person to absorb the benefits of the session while gradually returning to individual awareness. Practitioners visualize the group's light gently dissipating, sending any remaining energy outward as a blessing to all beings. This grounding allows each participant to leave the session feeling balanced, connected, and aligned with the Arcturian light.

Through these group practices, practitioners experience the profound impact of shared energy, a force that enhances each person's connection to Arcturian wisdom and amplifies their collective intentions. The circle becomes a space of mutual support and spiritual growth, a meeting point where individual energies blend into a harmonious whole. In each session, practitioners feel a deepened connection to the Arcturian presence, sensing that their shared efforts extend beyond the immediate group, touching the broader world with healing and light.

As practitioners continue their journey in these group settings, they recognize that the strength of their connection grows through each shared experience. The energy generated within the circle becomes a source of inspiration, guiding them in both individual practice and collective work. The Arcturian guidance serves as a beacon, illuminating the path of unity, compassion, and spiritual expansion, where each moment shared enhances the journey toward higher consciousness and collective evolution.

Building on the foundation of shared practices, practitioners now explore more advanced techniques to cultivate a cohesive and powerful group energy. The Arcturians guide them through practices that deepen the group's connection, fostering a supportive environment where each participant's energy aligns with the collective, creating an amplified field for spiritual and energetic work. These techniques allow groups to harness the full potential of their combined energy, offering healing, transformation, and alignment for both participants and the wider world.

A core practice in advanced group work is "collective resonance," where participants harmonize their energies to create a singular, elevated vibration. To achieve this resonance, practitioners sit in a circular arrangement, holding a shared intention of unity and connection. They begin with synchronized breathing, drawing in a slow breath together, then releasing it in unison. As they repeat this breath cycle, they visualize their energy merging into a unified field, a gentle and radiant light that fills the space. This practice creates a deep sense of oneness, aligning each individual with the collective intention and creating a foundation for the session.

The use of "energy attunement" enhances this resonance further, allowing participants to align with the Arcturian frequencies collectively. Practitioners close their eyes and visualize a stream of Arcturian light descending into the circle, connecting each participant. This light resonates through the group, gently raising their frequency and harmonizing individual energies. Practitioners sense this attunement as a subtle shift, a feeling of elevation that opens each person to higher awareness. This shared resonance creates an environment where insights and healing flow effortlessly, fostering a space where each participant feels supported and aligned with the group's purpose.

Advanced group practices also involve a guided technique known as "heart coherence." Each participant focuses on their heart center, breathing gently and visualizing a soft light radiating from within. As they continue, they extend this light outward, connecting with the hearts of others in the circle. Practitioners feel their heart energy merging, creating a single, cohesive field of compassion and unity. This heart coherence serves as an anchor, aligning the group with Arcturian qualities of love, empathy, and balance. Practitioners experience this connection as a warm, gentle pulse that harmonizes their intentions, amplifying their capacity for healing and transformation.

To further strengthen the group's energy, practitioners are guided through a technique of "intention amplification." Each participant silently holds a personal intention for the session, such as self-healing, inner clarity, or alignment with higher purpose. In silence, they focus on this intention, feeling it expand within their heart. When ready, they visualize this intention merging with the intentions of others in the circle, creating a powerful collective focus. The Arcturian energy flows through the group, amplifying each intention, transforming individual goals into a unified field of purpose. Practitioners sense the combined power of these intentions, feeling a heightened energy that supports each person's journey while resonating as a unified whole.

Sound becomes a transformative tool in these advanced sessions, where specific tones or chants are used to elevate the group's vibration. The Arcturians encourage practitioners to select sounds that resonate with their collective intention—tones that evoke peace, healing, or balance. As participants chant or tone together, they create a harmonic frequency that lifts the group's energy field. Practitioners sense this sound vibrating through each cell, filling the circle with a luminous resonance. This use of sound draws the Arcturian presence closer, creating an elevated space where healing energies flow freely, enriching each participant's experience and supporting the group's alignment.

Another essential element in advanced group work is the "circle of reflection," a practice where practitioners support one another through compassionate listening and shared insights. After a session, each participant is invited to share their experiences, observations, or any intuitive impressions that arose. Others listen attentively, holding a space of non-judgment and openness. This reflective practice allows participants to gain deeper insights, recognizing shared themes or messages that resonate throughout the group. Practitioners often find that insights gained in this circle offer profound clarity, helping them to integrate personal revelations while strengthening the collective bond.

The technique of "collective grounding" brings each session to a close, allowing participants to anchor the energies they've experienced. Practitioners visualize roots extending from their feet deep into the earth, feeling a steady connection with the ground. They envision any residual energy flowing gently into the earth, leaving them calm, balanced, and clear. This grounding practice ensures that each person leaves the session fully integrated, carrying the benefits of the group work with them while releasing any excess energy. Through this grounding, practitioners maintain stability and harmony, feeling the lasting effects of the session in their daily lives.

These advanced group practices foster an experience of unity and mutual support that transcends the individual journey, inviting practitioners to witness their growth and transformation as part of a collective. The group becomes a microcosm of spiritual alignment, a living expression of Arcturian principles that ripples outward into the world. Each session deepens the connection between participants, creating a field where energies blend into a harmonious whole that benefits not only the group but the broader community.

Practitioners find that these advanced group practices amplify their spiritual growth, creating a space where they can experience the Arcturian presence more vividly, feel supported in their intentions, and witness profound shifts in awareness. The shared journey becomes a powerful catalyst for transformation, where each person's growth enriches the group, and the group's combined energy magnifies each individual's experience.

With each session, practitioners feel the depth of their connection to one another and to the Arcturian guidance that supports their work. This shared path of unity and expansion reflects the potential of collective energy, a journey that honors the wisdom of the Arcturians and the spirit of collaboration. Through these advanced practices, the group becomes a vessel of light, a source of healing, inspiration, and alignment that radiates outward, touching each participant and extending to the wider world with clarity and peace.

Chapter 19
Deep Meditation

The journey into deep meditation with Arcturian guidance opens pathways to elevated states of awareness, inviting practitioners to explore layers of consciousness that lie beyond ordinary perception. As they delve into advanced meditative practices, they enter a realm where time slows, thoughts quiet, and the essence of the self unfolds. Through these Arcturian-guided meditations, practitioners experience heightened clarity and inner peace, embracing a level of awareness that aligns with their higher purpose.

Practitioners begin by entering a state of profound relaxation, a foundational aspect of deep meditation. Guided by gentle breathing techniques, they close their eyes and allow the tension within their body to dissolve. With each inhale, they draw in calm and centered energy; with each exhale, they release all residual thoughts or emotions. The Arcturians emphasize that relaxation creates the ideal conditions for deep meditation, fostering openness and stillness that allows consciousness to expand naturally.

Once relaxed, practitioners focus on the technique of "progressive breath alignment," a practice that synchronizes the breath with the body's natural rhythm. Breathing slowly and deeply, they visualize each breath as a wave, gently filling the body and washing away any remaining tension. This rhythmic breathing connects practitioners to their heart center, a focal point of Arcturian guidance, where they begin to sense a warm, subtle energy expanding outward. Practitioners allow their awareness to rest on this energy, experiencing it as a steady pulse that attunes them to inner peace and prepares them for deeper levels of awareness.

An essential component of deep meditation is the cultivation of a "mindful stillness." Practitioners gently observe their thoughts without judgment or attachment, simply noting each thought as it arises and allowing it to pass like a cloud drifting through a clear sky. In this mindful state, they begin to notice the space between thoughts, a quiet, expansive presence that lies beneath the surface of the mind. This presence is where practitioners feel the influence of Arcturian guidance most strongly, a tranquil awareness that encourages them to enter a profound inner silence. Through continued practice, they come to recognize this stillness as a doorway to the deeper self, a state where insights and understanding naturally arise.

As practitioners deepen into meditation, they are guided to visualize a "pillar of light" extending from above, a radiant column of Arcturian energy descending through the crown chakra. This light flows down through the body, aligning each chakra with higher frequencies, dissolving any blockages, and enhancing the energy field. Practitioners feel the warmth and purity of this light filling their entire being, creating a sense of balance and calm. The Arcturians emphasize that this pillar of light acts as a conduit for spiritual connection, strengthening the bond between practitioner and higher realms, allowing them to access wisdom and healing energies that support their journey.

Within this state of heightened alignment, practitioners engage in the practice of "expanded awareness." Guided by the Arcturian presence, they allow their consciousness to extend outward, sensing the space that surrounds them and then reaching beyond the physical boundaries of the body. This expanded awareness opens practitioners to a feeling of unity with the environment, a sense that they are connected to all things. With each breath, they feel themselves merging with the energy around them, experiencing a profound oneness that dissolves the boundaries of self. In this expansive state, practitioners often receive intuitive insights or feel a gentle peace that is both grounding and uplifting.

The Arcturians also introduce practitioners to "multi-dimensional sensing," a practice that brings awareness to higher vibrational frequencies and subtle realms. As they settle into deep meditation, practitioners gently focus on any sensations, images, or impressions that may arise. This technique opens the doorway to multi-dimensional perception, where practitioners sense energies that transcend the physical plane, experiencing glimpses of Arcturian realms or symbolic images that resonate with their personal journey. This sensing is not about analyzing but about remaining receptive, trusting that each impression holds meaning and insight. Through these encounters, practitioners deepen their understanding of the spiritual dimensions and the supportive presence of the Arcturians.

To ground these experiences, practitioners engage in a closing practice known as "conscious re-centering." After exploring elevated states, they gently guide their awareness back to the breath, feeling the body's weight and presence. They visualize roots extending from their feet into the earth, drawing in stability and grounding. This grounding process is essential, as it brings the heightened energies from meditation into a stable, balanced state, allowing practitioners to integrate insights into daily life. With each grounding breath, they anchor the energy of the session, feeling a renewed sense of clarity and purpose as they conclude their meditation.

As practitioners continue with these advanced meditation techniques, they experience profound transformations in both their inner and outer lives. The practice of deep meditation nurtures a sense of serenity and presence, a clarity that influences their thoughts, emotions, and actions. The insights gained during these meditations illuminate the path forward, offering guidance on their spiritual journey and strengthening their connection to the Arcturian wisdom that supports their growth.

Through these deep meditative states, practitioners find themselves aligned with the essence of their being, sensing an inner light that reflects the peace, understanding, and unity within all things. This journey into stillness, guided by the Arcturian presence, becomes a path to self-discovery and transcendence, a return to the true self where each moment in meditation deepens their relationship with the infinite.

As practitioners continue their journey into deep meditation, they are introduced to advanced techniques that help them reach even more profound states of awareness. These practices guide them beyond the physical self, expanding consciousness to experience elevated realms of understanding and harmony. Under the guidance of the Arcturians, practitioners enter a meditative space where boundaries dissolve, insights emerge naturally, and they connect with the deeper spiritual currents that flow through life. This phase is not merely about finding inner peace but about accessing states of consciousness that transform perception and open pathways to multidimensional experiences.

At the heart of this advanced meditation is the technique of "transcendent breath." Practitioners begin by settling into a calm and receptive state, gently slowing their breath to deepen relaxation. With each inhale, they imagine drawing in light from higher realms, and with each exhale, they let go of any remaining tension, surrendering fully to the moment. This breath becomes a bridge, guiding them into a state where thoughts and sensations soften. In this surrendered space, practitioners feel themselves becoming one with the present, a timeless awareness that serves as a gateway to deeper meditative states.

From this quieted mind, practitioners are guided to visualize a "cosmic light field," a vast and luminous expanse that stretches infinitely in all directions. They envision themselves entering this field, allowing its radiant energy to envelop them. In this space, they feel a profound sense of expansion, as if they are part of something boundless. The Arcturian presence is subtle yet powerful here, offering guidance and support as practitioners release any sense of separateness. They are encouraged to rest within this light, sensing that they are one with the energy that flows through all existence. This cosmic field becomes a source of healing and clarity, dissolving mental and emotional boundaries, inviting practitioners to explore their consciousness with openness.

As they deepen into this state, practitioners experience "vibrational elevation," where their energy aligns with the higher frequencies of the Arcturian realms. They may feel sensations such as gentle tingling or warmth, signs that they are attuning to these elevated energies. The Arcturians guide practitioners to welcome these sensations, letting them flow through each cell, harmonizing their entire being. This elevated vibration allows practitioners to reach a state of resonance where they are open to receiving wisdom from realms beyond the physical. In this heightened awareness, they often gain insights that reveal deeper truths, experiences that carry a sense of profound inner knowing.

Practitioners are also introduced to "expanded inner vision," a practice that encourages them to perceive beyond their physical senses. In this deep meditative state, they gently focus their awareness on the third eye, sensing the space within and around them. They may receive images, symbols, or colors, each holding meaning unique to their journey. Rather than analyzing these impressions, practitioners are guided to trust and observe, allowing the symbols to reveal their messages naturally. Through this inner vision, they perceive energies, patterns, and connections that offer insight into their spiritual path. Practitioners find that this expanded perception brings clarity and understanding that extend beyond the meditation, influencing how they view the world and their purpose within it.

In this phase of meditation, practitioners may also engage in "soul alignment," where they connect deeply with their own higher self, sensing the pure essence of their being. They visualize a stream of light connecting their heart with the infinite, a connection that feels timeless and profoundly intimate. As they rest in this alignment, they experience an awareness of their soul's purpose and the interconnectedness of all life. The Arcturians emphasize that this alignment is a powerful source of guidance and strength, a reminder of the wisdom and love that resides within. This practice allows practitioners to sense their true nature, a light that transcends the limitations of the physical self, bringing a lasting sense of peace and fulfillment.

For grounding these elevated experiences, practitioners conclude with a technique known as "anchoring presence." After exploring these higher states, they gently bring their focus back to their physical body, feeling their breath and the weight of their body against the surface on which they sit. They visualize roots extending from their base, anchoring them into the earth, feeling stable and centered. This anchoring presence ensures that the insights and energies gained during meditation integrate fully into the practitioner's everyday awareness, allowing them to carry the benefits of deep meditation into all aspects of life.

Through this advanced practice of deep meditation, practitioners come to experience the vastness of their consciousness and the serenity that arises from expanded awareness. Each meditative journey offers glimpses into the multidimensional nature of existence, where time, space, and identity dissolve into a sense of oneness. Practitioners find that these experiences gradually reshape their perception, opening them to a world where every moment carries depth, insight, and peace.

This journey into the depths of meditation, guided by the Arcturians, becomes a path of self-discovery and transcendence, a return to the true self. Practitioners emerge from each session with a renewed sense of clarity, inner strength, and a profound awareness of their connection to the universe.

Chapter 20
Advanced Channeling

In the depths of channeling, practitioners enter a space where communication flows from realms beyond the physical, a bridge to the wisdom of the Arcturians and other benevolent energies. Advanced channeling techniques refine this skill, transforming practitioners into clear conduits for messages that resonate with purpose and clarity. Through precise focus, intentional alignment, and inner discernment, they cultivate the capacity to receive detailed guidance while maintaining a state of balance and ethical mindfulness.

Practitioners begin by preparing the mind and body for channeling, using breath and visualization to calm any mental activity. They imagine a soft, radiant light enveloping their mind, dissolving thoughts and bringing stillness. With each inhalation, they deepen into a receptive state, creating a spaciousness within that allows for the unimpeded flow of guidance. This state of mental quiet becomes a sanctuary where messages can emerge naturally, free from interference by personal thoughts or emotions. Practitioners soon realize that this quieted mind becomes their greatest ally, an open field where Arcturian messages unfold with clarity and ease.

The foundation of advanced channeling lies in a practice known as "energetic coherence." Practitioners align with their heart center, visualizing a soft, warm light expanding outward. They allow this light to fill their entire being, creating a field of coherence that harmonizes the body, mind, and spirit. This state of inner harmony serves as a bridge, aligning their energy with the Arcturian frequencies. As they enter this state, they feel a subtle yet distinct resonance, an alignment with the wisdom they are about to channel. This coherence is essential; it grounds practitioners in the present moment, making them receptive to messages that resonate with the Arcturian essence of compassion and higher purpose.

With their inner alignment established, practitioners focus on the third-eye center, allowing their awareness to expand into a gentle, open receptivity. Here, they engage in a technique known as "intentional tuning," where they set a clear intention to receive only messages aligned with the highest good. This intention acts as a filter, guiding the flow of communication and ensuring that only benevolent energies connect through the channeling process. Practitioners hold this intention firmly yet gently, feeling it as a quiet assurance that shapes the quality of their experience. They know that each intention strengthens the clarity of the channel, allowing only insights that resonate with truth and integrity.

As they deepen into this receptive state, practitioners are encouraged to focus on "message discernment," a practice that helps them differentiate Arcturian messages from personal thoughts. They remain aware of subtle qualities in the communication—Arcturian messages often carry a distinct calm, depth, or lightness that practitioners come to recognize. Practitioners observe each word, image, or impression with an open mind, noting how it resonates. Through repeated practice, they develop a keen sense of what is authentic and aligned with Arcturian wisdom versus what may be influenced by their own mind. This discernment grows as a natural sensitivity, a subtle yet powerful awareness that sharpens with each session.

The Arcturians introduce practitioners to "energy shielding," a technique that ensures their energy remains stable and protected throughout the channeling process. Before each session, practitioners visualize a radiant shield surrounding their energy field, a boundary of light that filters out disruptive or misaligned influences. This shield maintains the purity of their connection, creating a safe and elevated space where messages can be received without interference. Practitioners feel a reassuring strength in this boundary, a field that both protects and amplifies the clarity of their channeling. Through this shielding, they feel secure, knowing that they are connected to an energy of trust and support.

In this secure and aligned space, practitioners engage in "guided inquiry," a practice of open-ended questions that invites clarity and depth in the guidance they receive. They may ask questions such as, "What insights are there for my current journey?" or "How can I align more deeply with my purpose?" Practitioners allow these questions to flow naturally, trusting that the Arcturians will respond in a way that resonates with their needs. Each question becomes a doorway, a point of focus that allows specific messages to emerge with precision. Practitioners remain patient and receptive, allowing the answers to arise in whatever form they may—words, images, sensations, or emotions. This openness to all forms of response creates a fuller channeling experience, one that honors the subtle and multidimensional nature of Arcturian communication.

As they receive these messages, practitioners are encouraged to engage in "focused anchoring," a practice where they gently repeat key insights or phrases to reinforce their understanding. Practitioners may softly repeat the words of guidance they receive, allowing them to resonate within their heart and mind. This repetition deepens their connection with the message, embedding it into their awareness in a way that makes it accessible beyond the session. Practitioners find that this anchoring process allows them to absorb the guidance fully, making it easier to integrate insights into daily life.

At the close of each session, practitioners perform "conscious disconnection," a gentle closing ritual where they bring their awareness back to the present moment and consciously release the channeling state. They express gratitude for the guidance received, feeling a sense of completion. Practitioners visualize the energy of the session flowing outward as a blessing, sending any residual energy into the universe with gratitude. They then focus on their breath, grounding themselves fully, feeling their presence within the physical body. This disconnection is as essential as the channeling itself, allowing practitioners to return to their everyday state of awareness with clarity and balance.

As practitioners advance in their channeling practice, they sense a growing relationship with the Arcturian guidance that flows through them. They become attuned to the language of light, the resonance of peace, and the depths of wisdom that each message carries. The practice of advanced channeling reveals itself as a path of continuous learning, where each session brings new layers of understanding and alignment. Practitioners feel empowered, knowing that they are connected to a higher source that offers support, clarity, and inspiration.

Through each experience, practitioners realize that channeling is not only about receiving messages but about cultivating a life aligned with these insights. They find themselves guided in subtle, profound ways, feeling a closer bond with their purpose and a deeper understanding of their journey. The Arcturian guidance becomes more than communication—it becomes a living presence, a source of inspiration and transformation that illuminates the path of their highest self.

Having built a foundation in discernment and energy alignment, practitioners now explore more intricate aspects of channeling, deepening their relationship with the Arcturian presence. As they move further into this practice, they are guided through advanced techniques that sharpen their clarity and enrich the messages received, allowing each interaction to become a more precise and intentional conduit for wisdom. Here, practitioners learn not only to sustain their energetic stability but to navigate complex energies, discerning the subtle nuances that elevate their channeling to new dimensions of understanding and insight.

At this stage, practitioners are introduced to "frequency refinement," a technique that focuses on tuning their energy to a specific vibrational frequency that aligns more precisely with the Arcturian realm. By visualizing a bright, pure light flowing down through their crown, they raise their inner vibration to match that of the Arcturian frequencies. This state of resonance enhances the quality of messages received, reducing interference from mental patterns or lower energies. Practitioners often sense this shift as a heightened clarity, a space of inner quiet that becomes their anchor in each session.

One essential practice for clarity in channeling is "multi-layered discernment," where practitioners develop the skill to distinguish subtle variations in energy and tone within the messages they receive. Each layer of communication carries a unique energetic imprint, and through practice, practitioners become sensitive to these nuances. For example, they may notice that Arcturian messages carry a warmth and steadiness, while messages from their own mind may feel more rapid or fragmented. By paying close attention to these subtle distinctions, practitioners strengthen their ability to recognize the origin of each message, building trust in the authenticity of their channeling.

Practitioners are encouraged to use "directed inquiry," an approach that involves setting specific intentions to guide the channeling session. They may enter the session with questions that focus on areas of growth, healing, or spiritual development, shaping the session's direction and deepening its relevance. By focusing their inquiries, practitioners engage in a dialogue that becomes more than passive listening—it transforms into an active exchange. As they focus on specific themes, they allow the Arcturian presence to offer guidance that is clear, practical, and aligned with their journey. This practice of directed inquiry enriches the experience, as each session becomes a step forward in understanding and evolution.

A powerful technique introduced at this stage is "energy stabilization," which practitioners use to maintain a consistent frequency throughout the channeling process, even when complex energies arise. Practitioners visualize an orb of light at their heart center, a stable source of energy that grounds them regardless of fluctuations in the channeling experience. This inner stability allows them to remain centered, preventing any outside influences or sudden surges in energy from disrupting their focus. Through this stabilized presence, practitioners can engage with more intricate messages without losing their balance, maintaining a calm that enhances the clarity and depth of the channeling.

"Temporal alignment" is another advanced technique practiced here, where practitioners learn to extend their awareness beyond the linear flow of time. This process opens a doorway to insights that transcend past, present, and future, as Arcturian guidance often comes from a perspective that encompasses multiple timelines. Practitioners enter this space by relaxing their focus on time, allowing insights to arise without the boundaries of immediate relevance. Through this state, they may gain revelations that apply not only to their current life phase but to long-term spiritual evolution. This expanded awareness enables practitioners to understand their journey in a broader context, accessing guidance that helps them align with their purpose across multiple dimensions.

An essential part of advanced channeling is the practice of "message integration," where practitioners consciously absorb and incorporate each message's essence. Upon receiving a message, they allow it to resonate within, feeling its truth resonate at an intuitive level. This integration process is gentle and reflective; practitioners do not rush but let each message find its place within their understanding. Through this process, they begin to embody the guidance they receive, creating a bridge between wisdom and daily practice. Practitioners find that this embodiment allows insights to naturally influence their actions and decisions, transforming channeling from an isolated experience into an integrated way of being.

To conclude each session, practitioners practice "conscious release," a grounding technique that ensures they transition smoothly from the heightened state of channeling back to everyday awareness. They visualize themselves surrounded by light, feeling a gentle pull toward the earth, grounding the energy of the session within their body. This grounding is essential, anchoring them in the present moment and allowing the insights to settle into their consciousness without overwhelm. As they return to their regular state of awareness, they express gratitude for the guidance received, knowing that each session strengthens their connection to the Arcturian wisdom they hold within.

Through these advanced practices, practitioners experience channeling as a dynamic relationship, one that grows in depth and clarity with each session. The guidance they receive becomes a living presence, a source of both wisdom and peace that gently transforms their perspective. Each insight gained strengthens their sense of purpose, illuminating their path forward with renewed understanding and trust.

The journey of advanced channeling reveals itself as an ongoing evolution, a journey where each experience builds upon the last, expanding practitioners' awareness and aligning them more deeply with the Arcturian light. They come to see channeling not only as a practice but as a connection to a greater purpose, one that inspires and empowers them on their path of spiritual growth and healing.

Chapter 21
Earth Healing

In the heart of the Arcturian teachings lies a profound reverence for Earth as a living being, a sanctuary that sustains all life and connects humanity to the cosmos. The Arcturians guide practitioners to cultivate an awareness of Earth's energy, inviting them into a partnership where healing flows not only to individuals but to the planet itself.

The journey into Earth healing begins with an immersion into the concept of Earth's energy field, an interconnected web that pulses through the soil, water, plants, animals, and beyond. Practitioners are guided to feel their own connection to this field, recognizing how it mirrors the body's energy centers. Through grounding practices, they tune into the steady rhythm of Earth, sensing its cycles and its presence beneath their feet. Practitioners visualize roots extending from their body, connecting deeply into Earth's core, and as they breathe, they draw in its strength and stability, anchoring themselves within its nurturing embrace. This grounding becomes the foundation upon which all planetary healing rests.

With their awareness attuned, practitioners are introduced to "planetary resonance," a technique that aligns their personal energy with Earth's natural vibrations. Practitioners close their eyes, sensing the hum of life beneath them, a vibration that resonates softly yet powerfully. They synchronize their breathing with this pulse, entering a state of deep resonance. In this state, they feel a kinship with Earth's elements, sensing how their own energy field merges with the larger field around them. This connection not only deepens their empathy for Earth's well-being but also prepares them to channel healing energy effectively and with pure intention.

Guided by the Arcturian presence, practitioners are then led into the practice of "elemental attunement," where they focus on connecting with the core elements of Earth—earth, water, fire, and air. Each element carries its own frequency, and practitioners learn to honor and align with these forces, sensing how they contribute to Earth's balance. They visualize each element within themselves, starting with the grounding stability of earth, then the fluidity of water, the transformative power of fire, and the life-sustaining essence of air. Through this inner attunement, they cultivate a holistic understanding of Earth's systems and recognize their role within these natural cycles.

An integral aspect of Earth healing is "energetic offering," a practice where practitioners channel healing energy to specific regions or ecosystems in need. With clear intention, they visualize a golden light forming within their heart, representing compassion and healing. They guide this light downward, sending it through their body and into the Earth, allowing it to flow toward places they feel may benefit from support. Practitioners trust that this energy travels intuitively, guided by the Arcturian presence to locations where it is most needed. They may focus on an area affected by environmental imbalance or visualize light infusing a natural landscape, revitalizing it with harmony and strength.

A deeper layer of this practice introduces "ecological empathy," where practitioners attune to the feelings and needs of Earth itself, perceiving its subtle messages. This practice requires them to enter a receptive state, quieting the mind and opening the heart to sense Earth's rhythms and signals. They listen beyond words, feeling impressions that convey Earth's vitality and areas in need of healing. Practitioners may experience a sense of warmth or coolness, colors, or symbols that represent Earth's current state. Through this empathy, they gain a more intuitive understanding of Earth's needs, allowing them to direct healing energy with greater precision and respect.

To enhance these practices, practitioners engage in "ceremonial grounding," a ritual that honors Earth as a sacred presence and reinforces their commitment to its well-being. They create a simple space outdoors, surrounded by natural elements, and focus their energy on gratitude. Practitioners may place their hands on the ground, feeling Earth's steady pulse beneath them, and express appreciation for all it provides. This ritual creates a deep, ceremonial connection, affirming their role as guardians of the planet's energy. It serves as a reminder that Earth healing is a partnership, one in which each individual contributes to the whole with reverence and love.

At the conclusion of each Earth healing session, practitioners perform a grounding practice known as "rooted gratitude." Having directed energy to the planet, they refocus on their own bodies, feeling the support of the ground beneath them. They visualize any remaining energy flowing from their heart into the Earth as a final offering, grounding their experience in appreciation and humility. Through this closing practice, they honor the reciprocal relationship they hold with Earth, releasing the energy with gratitude and respect.

As practitioners engage in these Earth healing practices, they begin to feel a shift within themselves—a deepened connection to the natural world and a heightened sense of purpose. Each act of healing becomes a prayer of gratitude, a moment of unity where they realize that their well-being is intertwined with Earth's. They sense the presence of the Arcturians guiding them, instilling a reverence for the planet that fosters both healing and a renewed awareness of their role as stewards.

Earth healing, under the guidance of the Arcturians, transforms into a practice that extends beyond individual intent. Practitioners experience a calling to care for the planet not only as inhabitants but as co-creators in its thriving, honoring its beauty, resilience, and life-giving energy. Through each act of healing, they join a lineage of light that supports Earth's journey, sensing that their energy, aligned with the Arcturian presence, flows as a force of renewal and balance.

In the second phase of Earth healing, practitioners deepen their connection to the planet through advanced techniques, learning to anchor Arcturian energies in specific places, ecosystems, or even global energy grids.

At the heart of this advanced practice is the "energy anchoring" technique, where practitioners focus on channeling Arcturian light into precise locations or ecosystems that would benefit from support. Guided by their intuition, they visualize a stream of vibrant light descending from above, flowing into the chosen site. This light is not only healing but harmonizing, adapting to the needs of each place it touches. Practitioners sense this energy integrating into the earth, permeating soil, water, and air, leaving a lasting impression that aligns the area with balance and renewal.

Building on this, practitioners engage in "sacred site alignment," a practice that focuses on areas of natural power—forests, mountains, rivers, or even cultural landmarks that hold significant spiritual energy. They connect with these sacred sites remotely or in person, sensing the unique vibrational quality of each place. Practitioners imagine a continuous energy link between themselves and the site, strengthening it with Arcturian light. As they tune into this resonance, they become aware of Earth's natural energetic pathways, recognizing how each site contributes to the planetary grid. This alignment practice not only fortifies the energy of sacred places but enhances their capacity to radiate healing across greater distances.

The Arcturians introduce practitioners to "grid harmonization," where they work with Earth's energetic grid, often referred to as ley lines, which act as conduits of energy flowing across the planet. By visualizing these lines as pathways of light, practitioners imagine themselves connecting to them, amplifying their energy through intention. They envision Arcturian light moving along these lines, bringing harmony to each intersecting point, known as a node. This practice strengthens the Earth's energy system, balancing areas that may be misaligned and creating a greater sense of planetary cohesion.

In this phase, practitioners are also guided to perform "collective healing meditations," where they join their energy with others to amplify the impact of their work. Practitioners visualize themselves as part of a network of individuals connected through a shared intention to support Earth. Together, they create a field of light that spans vast areas, sending healing energy to ecosystems, weather systems, or areas experiencing environmental challenges. The collective focus heightens the effectiveness of the practice, allowing their combined energies to ripple through the earth, reaching places that may need profound restoration and support.

An essential element of this advanced Earth healing is "planetary attunement," where practitioners align their energy with the seasonal cycles, lunar phases, and other natural rhythms. They work with these cycles as times of enhanced receptivity, allowing their healing efforts to blend seamlessly with the natural flow of Earth's energies. For example, they might attune to the energy of the spring equinox, a time of growth and renewal, to reinforce regrowth in areas affected by deforestation. Or, they may synchronize their practice with the full moon, amplifying their energy and intentions to strengthen ecosystems under stress. This attunement brings a deeper awareness of Earth's needs and enhances the effectiveness of their work.

Practitioners also learn "ecosystem resonance," a practice where they focus on tuning into specific ecosystems, such as forests, rivers, or oceans. By sensing the unique qualities of each ecosystem, they become aware of its vitality, balance, and any areas that may feel depleted. Practitioners extend Arcturian energy into these spaces, visualizing it as a restorative force that blends seamlessly with each element—water flowing with light, plants absorbing warmth, and air filled with healing frequencies. This resonance attunes practitioners to the interconnectedness of all life, fostering a sense of unity and shared vitality.

As practitioners bring each Earth healing session to a close, they perform "grounding through gratitude," a technique that allows them to release and integrate the energy they have worked with. Practitioners imagine their energy flowing back into their own bodies, anchoring any remaining vibrations within, while expressing deep gratitude for Earth and the opportunity to serve as stewards. They acknowledge the symbiotic relationship between humanity and the planet, sensing a lasting bond that transcends the practice itself. This grounding strengthens their own energy field, allowing them to carry the effects of each session into daily life with humility and respect.

In embracing these advanced Earth healing practices, practitioners find that their connection to the planet transforms into a living partnership, a continuous flow of giving and receiving that nurtures both Earth and themselves. Each session enhances their sense of purpose, knowing they contribute to a force greater than themselves, a legacy of healing that ripples through time and space. The Arcturian guidance in these practices becomes a beacon, illuminating the path of harmony and care that each practitioner carries forward, creating a future where the planet and its inhabitants thrive as one.

Chapter 22
Daily Practice

In the journey of connecting with the Arcturians, one of the most profound insights is that spirituality is not confined to specific moments but can flow through every aspect of daily life. Here, the Arcturians introduce practitioners to practices that weave their energy into the fabric of the everyday, cultivating a steady state of connection, balance, and presence. These daily practices are designed to serve as touchpoints throughout the day, gentle reminders of the Arcturian energy that supports growth and harmony, no matter where life's demands may lead.

Practitioners begin with the "Morning Alignment Ritual," a simple yet powerful practice that sets an intentional tone for the day. Upon waking, they close their eyes and focus on their breath, feeling the steady rise and fall as they reconnect with their inner self. Visualizing a stream of Arcturian light descending from above, they allow this energy to gently fill their body, creating a soft, radiant field around them. This morning ritual not only aligns their energy with a higher frequency but also serves as a reminder that they carry the Arcturian presence with them throughout the day. Practitioners feel this light offering strength and clarity, preparing them for whatever the day may bring.

Throughout their day, practitioners engage in "mindful breathing," a practice that connects them with Arcturian energy at any moment, no matter where they are. When they feel tension or distraction, they take a few conscious breaths, visualizing each inhale as a wave of calming energy and each exhale as a release of tension. This simple act centers them in the present moment, clearing the mind and refreshing the body. By incorporating mindful breathing into daily routines, practitioners create brief but profound pauses where they can reset and reconnect with a sense of purpose and peace, subtly infusing the day with a steady, balanced energy.

Another essential technique is the "Heart Center Focus," where practitioners place their hands over their heart, breathing slowly and deeply as they center their awareness in this space. The Arcturians emphasize that the heart is a powerful center for spiritual energy, and by focusing here, practitioners feel a warmth and calm that spreads through their entire being. This practice can be done before important interactions, grounding practitioners in compassion and clarity. Through this technique, they find themselves more open and present, able to approach each situation from a place of love and understanding, aligning with the Arcturian intention of harmony.

Practitioners are encouraged to engage in the "Midday Reset," a brief session designed to restore energy during the day. They close their eyes, take a few deep breaths, and visualize themselves bathed in a sphere of Arcturian light. In this protective space, they feel any stress or distractions dissolve, replaced by a renewed sense of vitality and focus. This midday practice serves as an opportunity to clear any accumulated energies, maintaining a sense of clarity and alignment as they move into the latter half of the day.

An integral part of these daily practices is "Intentional Awareness," where practitioners consciously bring the Arcturian energy into their everyday interactions. Before entering a conversation or beginning a task, they take a moment to pause, setting an intention for the interaction to unfold in harmony and understanding. This small act invites a subtle but transformative energy, helping practitioners remain mindful of their influence and creating spaces that reflect peace and kindness. This awareness fosters connections that are authentic and respectful, deepening their sense of connection not only with others but with the Arcturian presence that guides them.

Before the day concludes, practitioners engage in an "Evening Reflection" to release the day's energies and realign with a sense of inner peace. In a quiet space, they close their eyes, breathing deeply and reflecting on the moments that stood out to them. They visualize each experience surrounded by light, honoring any lessons or insights gained. Practitioners express gratitude for these experiences, letting go of any lingering energy that may no longer serve them. This reflection allows them to enter a state of rest with a sense of closure and peace, reconnecting with the Arcturian presence as they prepare for sleep.

As they settle in, practitioners end the day with a "Nightly Grounding" practice, where they visualize roots extending from their body, anchoring deep into Earth's core. They feel any remaining energy of the day flow downward, grounding and balancing them. This grounding reinforces stability, allowing practitioners to rest without carrying the day's energies into the night. Through this process, they enter sleep with a calm, open heart, sensing the gentle support of the Arcturians surrounding them as they drift into rest.

By integrating these practices into daily life, practitioners experience a transformation in how they approach each moment, viewing the day as a series of opportunities to connect with their purpose and the energies of peace and alignment. The influence of the Arcturian presence becomes a steady force, a source of inspiration and strength that guides them with subtle grace. Each breath, each pause, and each reflection becomes part of a rhythm that weaves spirituality into the simplest actions, creating a life where the essence of the Arcturian energy flows seamlessly throughout the day.

As practitioners delve further into daily integration, they explore additional techniques that ground the Arcturian energy within their daily routines, cultivating a consistent rhythm of spiritual connection and growth. These practices are not meant to separate the sacred from the mundane but to reveal how every action, when infused with intention, becomes a channel for

Arcturian guidance and support. In this expanded phase, practitioners discover advanced methods for adapting these energies to life's daily challenges, building resilience, and nurturing a deep inner calm that remains steady regardless of external circumstances.

A key technique in this phase is the "Protective Energy Field," a practice that creates a boundary of light around the practitioner, enhancing both clarity and stability throughout the day. Upon waking or before stepping into new environments, they visualize a protective sphere of Arcturian light surrounding them. This light acts as both a filter and a shield, allowing beneficial energies to flow freely while filtering out discordant vibrations. Practitioners experience this shield not as separation but as a soft boundary that nurtures their energy. This practice reinforces their sense of inner peace, making it easier to maintain clarity in situations that might otherwise disrupt their balance.

Another valuable technique is "Moment-to-Moment Presence," an approach where practitioners use each action, no matter how routine, as an opportunity to bring awareness and intention to the present moment. As they wash dishes, walk to work, or listen to others, they focus on the sensation, rhythm, and energy of the experience itself. Practitioners feel the Arcturian presence within each moment, noticing how awareness transforms ordinary actions into something more—a form of meditation, a reflection of peace, and a quiet space for receiving insights. Through this practice, they come to realize that spirituality is not separate from their everyday lives but is woven into each breath, thought, and action.

Practitioners also explore the practice of "Energy Refreshing," a method for rebalancing and realigning in moments when they feel drained or distracted. They visualize a fresh stream of Arcturian energy flowing down from above, revitalizing each energy center as it moves through their body. This light dissolves any dense or stagnant energy, clearing their mind and restoring focus. Practitioners find this practice especially helpful after intense situations or challenging conversations, as it provides an instant realignment that allows them to return to their day with renewed vitality.

A powerful addition to their routine is the practice of "Intentional Gratitude." Before meals, before meetings, or in moments of pause, practitioners take a brief moment to focus on something they are grateful for. By tuning into this gratitude, they open themselves to a higher frequency, which elevates their energy and aligns them with the Arcturian essence of appreciation and abundance. Practitioners discover that this practice enriches each experience, deepening their sense of connection to the present and helping them cultivate a positive outlook that influences their day.

To further integrate Arcturian practices into the evening, practitioners engage in "Review and Release," a quiet reflection on their day's experiences. They recall moments that brought joy, insights, or challenges, visualizing these experiences surrounded by light. They honor these moments, feeling gratitude for each one, knowing it has contributed to their growth. Practitioners allow any remaining energy to be released, visualizing it flowing out of their body and into the earth. This practice clears their field, allowing them to enter a state of rest free from any lingering energy or tension from the day.

A final step in this evening routine is the "Heart Light Expansion," where practitioners place their hands over their heart and visualize a gentle, radiant light within. They sense this light expanding outward, filling their entire body and space around them. This heart-centered energy serves as a final grounding before sleep, creating a sense of warmth and peace. They feel the Arcturian presence surrounding them, offering protection and comfort as they enter the dream state. Practitioners often find that this practice enhances the quality of their rest, helping them wake with clarity and focus.

Through these advanced practices, practitioners reach a level of integration where spiritual awareness flows naturally into every corner of their lives. The Arcturian presence becomes not only a part of their practice but an active presence that supports, guides, and enriches each moment. They begin to experience life as a series of interconnected moments, each filled with the potential for learning, peace, and alignment. With each mindful breath, each intention, and each act of gratitude, they cultivate a life aligned with their purpose, harmonizing with the Arcturian energies in a way that transforms their everyday experiences into pathways of light and consciousness.

Chapter 23
Spiritual Integration

In the path of spiritual development, there comes a time when learning and practice evolve into something deeper—a lasting transformation that becomes part of who one is. This stage of spiritual integration invites practitioners to weave together the various Arcturian teachings into a cohesive foundation, one that supports them consistently and with purpose. Rather than isolated practices, each technique, meditation, and insight flows into a unified experience that brings inner harmony and aligns one's life with the steady presence of Arcturian guidance.

This integration begins with "Inner Synthesis," a reflection on each Arcturian practice and the ways it has influenced the practitioner's journey. Practitioners are encouraged to observe how each aspect—self-healing, energy alignment, intuition, and collective healing—has deepened their sense of self and purpose. They visualize these practices as threads of light that weave together, forming a unified tapestry within. In this tapestry, each thread is interconnected, creating a resilient energy matrix that is rooted within them. Practitioners may feel a shift in their energy as they recognize this internal harmony, allowing them to move forward with renewed clarity and understanding.

A central element of this phase is the practice of "Harmonized Life Vision," where practitioners tune into their highest intentions for their life path. This technique involves sitting in meditation and opening to the Arcturian presence, allowing visions, symbols, or impressions to emerge that represent their truest aspirations. Practitioners sense these visions as luminous, aligning with their inner purpose and bringing direction. They then bring these visions into focus, asking the Arcturian guidance to help them align their daily actions, relationships, and thoughts with this higher calling. This vision becomes a guiding light, a quiet yet powerful presence that anchors their spiritual progress into a sustainable path.

Practitioners also engage in "Energetic Anchoring," where they learn to embody Arcturian energy throughout their daily life. Through breathing exercises and visualization, they anchor this energy within specific aspects of their routine, such as morning reflections, moments of gratitude, or daily tasks. Practitioners imagine a bright Arcturian light filling these moments, making each a point of connection to their spiritual path. This integration allows them to feel the Arcturian guidance steadily, creating a life where every action—no matter how simple—reflects their spiritual awareness. This anchoring transforms their environment, radiating energy that nurtures both their surroundings and those they encounter.

Another transformative practice is "Arcturian Self-Alignment," where practitioners revisit the core values that resonate with their Arcturian journey. With guidance, they assess the values they hold dear—compassion, integrity, patience, resilience—and explore how these manifest in their lives. They may choose a single value to embody each week, focusing on how it flows through their actions and thoughts. Practitioners feel the Arcturian presence deepening this alignment, enhancing their capacity to live authentically. This alignment builds a bridge between their inner growth and outer expression, transforming the spiritual journey into a way of being that touches every facet of life.

One of the most meaningful elements in this phase is "Integrative Stillness," where practitioners create moments of silent reflection that allow for internal processing and grounding. In quiet spaces, they let go of effort and simply rest in presence, feeling the Arcturian energy within. In this stillness, practitioners sense their experiences settling, the lessons and practices blending seamlessly. They feel a calm understanding that transcends words, a sense that everything they've learned exists within them in a balanced and unified way. This stillness serves as a reminder that their spiritual foundation is secure, allowing them to move forward without needing to force or strive.

As practitioners continue integrating these aspects, they develop a "Living Practice," where the Arcturian energy is ever-present, seamlessly flowing into their interactions, decisions, and self-reflections. With each day, they recognize how this integration creates a steady sense of purpose, allowing them to navigate life with resilience and clarity. Practitioners find that the Arcturian teachings are no longer just practices—they are embedded in how they respond to challenges, how they connect with others, and how they perceive themselves. This living practice shapes a life that is naturally attuned to spiritual growth and deeply aligned with their essence.

With each moment of integration, practitioners experience the Arcturian presence as a gentle and constant support, illuminating a path that is both inward and outward. The techniques and teachings become more than steps—they become a harmonious flow that carries them, resonating with their inner purpose and guiding them toward a life of meaning, compassion, and peace.

Deepening the journey of spiritual integration, practitioners are guided toward a reflective and intentional phase that allows them to truly anchor the Arcturian teachings within their daily existence.

Central to this phase is the practice of "Reflective Alignment," where practitioners are encouraged to revisit their spiritual path, assessing the impact of their practices on their personal growth and their interactions with the world. Sitting in quiet meditation, they bring awareness to the practices that resonate most deeply, noting any shifts in their perception, behaviors, or sense of self. As they reflect, they may feel a gentle Arcturian presence guiding them to identify areas of progress and areas for further development. This reflective alignment helps practitioners fine-tune their spiritual routines, fostering an environment where their energy remains balanced, purposeful, and attuned to their highest intentions.

Practitioners also engage in "Periodic Spiritual Review," a process of revisiting their spiritual goals and practices to ensure they align with their evolving values and insights. In this review, they explore questions such as: Are my practices still supporting my growth? Have new insights emerged that require deeper exploration? Guided by their inner intuition and Arcturian energy, they may find certain practices that need adaptation or others that can be embraced in new ways. This review process fosters a dynamic relationship with their spiritual journey, allowing them to remain fluid and open, embracing growth as a constant unfolding rather than a fixed destination.

Another key technique is "Life Harmonization," where practitioners learn to balance spiritual practices with the demands of daily life. Through visualization, they see themselves moving through daily activities while carrying a gentle Arcturian light within. They sense this light harmonizing their thoughts, emotions, and interactions, creating an inner resonance that blends spirituality with everyday responsibilities. Practitioners recognize that spiritual integration does not require separation from the world but, instead, an approach that brings peace, clarity, and presence into every aspect of life. This harmonization becomes a steady rhythm that maintains their spiritual connection, whether in moments of solitude or during the busyness of daily routines.

In deepening their connection, practitioners are introduced to "Sacred Reconnection," a practice where they regularly return to core Arcturian techniques—such as meditation, self-alignment, and energy balancing—to refresh and renew their spiritual energy. This reconnection serves as a reminder of the foundational principles of their path, providing a space to rest, recharge, and restore clarity. By engaging in this sacred reconnection, practitioners find their energies rejuvenated and their commitment renewed, sensing that each return deepens their connection with the Arcturian guidance that has supported them throughout their journey.

A significant part of this stage is "Personal Integration Ritual," a practice developed by each practitioner to honor their journey and align with their highest intentions. Practitioners are encouraged to create a personalized ritual that reflects their unique path, such as lighting a candle, writing reflections, or meditating at a specific time each week. This ritual becomes a touchstone, a sacred moment where they consciously honor their progress, release any unnecessary energies, and reaffirm their commitment to inner growth. Through this personalized ritual, practitioners cultivate a deep sense of ownership over their path, fostering a lifelong connection to the Arcturian guidance that has become part of their essence.

Practitioners then explore "Living Intention," where they set clear, focused intentions that guide them as they move forward. In a meditative state, they invite the Arcturian presence to inspire and clarify these intentions, feeling the subtle energy shift as they align with their inner truth. They might choose intentions related to compassion, presence, or resilience, allowing these to guide their thoughts, actions, and responses. This practice of living with intention creates a steady compass, one that aligns with both their personal goals and the greater flow of universal energy, anchoring their life in purpose and meaning.

As practitioners continue through this phase, they experience spiritual integration not as an end but as a living journey, where each moment of alignment brings them closer to the essence of their being. The Arcturian teachings become embedded in their perception, guiding them gently in times of joy and challenge alike. In this phase of integration, practitioners find a quiet and profound transformation, where spirituality merges seamlessly with everyday life, creating a foundation that supports not only their own growth but the growth of those around them. Through each intention, each reflection, and each return to their core, they cultivate a life that resonates with harmony, purpose, and the enduring light of the Arcturian presence.

Chapter 24
Collective Journey

In the spiritual path toward higher consciousness, there exists a profound realization that one's growth is interconnected with the evolution of all beings. The Arcturians introduce the concept of the collective journey, a shared path where individual growth is amplified by and contributes to the transformation of the wider community. One of the primary practices in this collective journey is "Unified Intention Setting," where practitioners gather—physically or energetically—and focus on a shared intention for healing, harmony, or insight. Sitting in a circle, either in person or remotely, practitioners connect with the Arcturian presence, feeling its energy weaving among them, creating a strong bond of mutual support. As they set their collective intention, they visualize this intention as a radiant light, building with each participant's energy until it forms a powerful, unified field. This practice enhances the impact of their intentions, creating a supportive space that extends beyond the individual to the collective.

Another significant aspect of this journey is "Group Resonance Meditation," a technique where participants align their energies through synchronized breathing and visualization. In this meditation, practitioners focus on the breath, breathing as one, and then visualize a shared light that flows through each participant, creating a harmonious and expansive field. They feel this energy resonate and amplify within the group, reaching out beyond their circle to bring harmony to the surrounding environment. The group resonance meditation fosters a deep connection, not only to the Arcturian presence but to each other, instilling a sense of unity and a shared purpose that strengthens each individual's practice.

Practitioners are also introduced to "Collective Heart Coherence," a powerful technique in which the group collectively centers their energy in the heart space, cultivating feelings of compassion, gratitude, and peace. As they synchronize their heart energy, practitioners visualize the energy radiating outward, expanding beyond the immediate group to touch those around them and the Earth itself. This practice transforms the energy field of the group, creating an atmosphere of profound peace and openness. Participants feel the Arcturian guidance gently enhancing this coherence, as if connecting each heart with a thread of light that fosters both individual and collective healing.

An essential part of this collective journey is "Supportive Energy Exchange," where practitioners offer and receive energy within the group. In this practice, participants take turns focusing on one individual, sending supportive Arcturian energy to them through visualization and intention. The person receiving this energy experiences a sense of warmth and alignment as the group's collective energy surrounds and uplifts them. This supportive exchange creates a profound experience of connection, reinforcing the idea that spiritual growth is not a solitary endeavor but a shared journey where individuals uplift and inspire one another.

To anchor these collective practices, practitioners engage in "Sacred Group Reflection," a technique where they reflect together on insights, experiences, and realizations. In a circle, each participant shares their personal journey, thoughts, or feelings, with the others holding space in compassionate silence. This reflection allows practitioners to witness and support each other's progress, fostering a sense of belonging and mutual respect. Guided by the Arcturian energy, participants feel a deeper understanding of their collective role, recognizing that their personal growth contributes to the elevation of the whole group.

Another vital component in this phase is "Collective Healing Intention," where the group channels their energies toward a shared goal, such as environmental healing, community support, or global peace. In this practice, participants visualize their combined energy forming a beam of Arcturian light, directed toward a specific cause or location. As they focus on this intention, they feel their energy merging with the Arcturian presence, which amplifies their intention and guides it toward the intended goal. This practice deepens the awareness of their collective power, fostering a commitment to use their abilities for the benefit of the broader world.

Through each of these collective practices, practitioners find that their individual experiences blend into a shared journey of discovery and transformation. The collective path becomes a living embodiment of the Arcturian guidance, a reminder that every individual's growth is interconnected with the evolution of the whole. In participating fully, practitioners experience a profound alignment with others and with the universe, sensing the collective journey as a sacred unfolding that strengthens, heals, and elevates all involved.

Building upon the collective practices introduced, practitioners now deepen their engagement with group energy, focusing on techniques that foster unity, mutual support, and expanded healing. This phase offers tools for facilitating collective spiritual experiences, creating an environment where Arcturian energy flows freely within a group, amplifying its effects and reaching beyond individual boundaries. Here, practitioners learn that the power of a group transcends the sum of its parts, forming a collective consciousness that enhances spiritual evolution for all involved.

A profound practice in this stage is "Energy Harmonization," where practitioners align the group's energies through synchronized visualization. In this technique, each person envisions themselves as a vessel of Arcturian light, feeling the energy flowing through them and connecting with others in the group. This light begins to expand, interweaving with each participant's energy to form a unified field. As this field grows stronger, practitioners sense a harmonious vibration that brings stability and resonance, creating a powerful collective space. This harmonization forms a foundation that allows each member to access deeper layers of consciousness, fostering an environment of mutual healing and inspiration.

An essential aspect of this practice is "Group Grounding," where practitioners work to anchor the group's collective energy into the Earth. Each participant visualizes roots extending from their feet into the Earth, connecting with its energy. This grounding allows the group to feel steady and connected, maintaining balance during intense spiritual work. The Arcturian energy is felt flowing through these roots, stabilizing the group and ensuring that the work they undertake together remains grounded in a calm, centered foundation. This technique becomes particularly valuable during collective healing sessions, ensuring that each participant is energetically secure and aligned.

To facilitate meaningful group interactions, practitioners are introduced to "Sacred Listening Circles," a practice that emphasizes the power of listening with presence and empathy. Participants take turns speaking, while the others listen deeply, holding space with compassion and without judgment. In these circles, individuals share insights, challenges, or inspirations, creating a safe environment for authentic expression. This practice strengthens trust within the group, allowing each member to feel seen and heard, and reinforcing the understanding that collective energy thrives on openness and shared respect. Through sacred listening, practitioners discover that group connection is as much about receiving as it is about giving, fostering a balance that enriches all.

Practitioners also engage in "Shared Visioning," where the group collectively envisions a harmonious world or a specific healing outcome. In this guided visualization, each member imagines their ideal vision, seeing it vividly as if it has already come to fruition. They then merge their vision with that of others, creating a shared image of peace, healing, or unity that fills the group's energy field. The Arcturian presence enhances this vision, amplifying its reach beyond the immediate group. Through shared visioning, practitioners contribute to a potent collective intention, reinforcing their role as co-creators of a world aligned with higher consciousness.

In this deepened phase, the group also explores "Collective Sacred Spaces," learning techniques for creating an energetically cleansed and consecrated environment. Practitioners prepare the space with intention, using Arcturian energy to clear any residual energies and establish a sacred atmosphere. Each participant contributes to the space's energy by visualizing a light from the Arcturian realm filling the room, creating a sanctuary where spiritual work is supported and elevated. This sacred space becomes a container for collective practices, enhancing the group's ability to connect and access higher frequencies, creating a field that feels both protected and expansive.

A significant practice in this stage is "Amplified Healing," where the group directs collective Arcturian energy toward a specific healing purpose. Practitioners gather in a circle, visualizing a central point within the group where they channel their energies. They focus on a chosen individual, group, or world issue, feeling the Arcturian light flowing through them and into this central point. The energy gathers, intensifying as it combines with each participant's intention. Practitioners witness the profound impact of their unified energy, sensing how collective healing becomes exponentially more powerful, as if each member's energy is enhanced by the synergy of the group.

Through these advanced practices, practitioners discover the profound potential of a collective journey. They feel a transformative resonance, a frequency that exists only when individuals come together with shared purpose and open hearts. Each practice not only strengthens their connection to the Arcturian energy but also deepens their bond with each other, creating a sense of unity that goes beyond words. In these shared experiences, practitioners witness the collective journey as a dynamic, living path, one that reflects the highest ideals of harmony, compassion, and universal alignment. This phase of collective work reinforces the understanding that spiritual evolution is an interconnected tapestry, woven from the energy, intentions, and hearts of all those who walk this path together.

Chapter 25
Social Projects

In the journey of spiritual evolution, there comes a natural calling to extend one's growth beyond the self, channeling energy into collective and social projects. Practitioners are introduced to the Arcturian perspective on using spiritual practices to benefit society, emphasizing that the energy cultivated in individual work can transform lives and uplift communities. They explore how to direct Arcturian energy into tangible social actions, merging spiritual insight with practical efforts to enhance well-being, harmony, and growth in the world around them.

Practitioners begin by developing the foundation of "Intentional Service," a practice of approaching social projects with a clear, focused intention of healing and support. In meditation, they connect with the Arcturian energy, visualizing it flowing from them to their chosen cause or group. They allow the Arcturian presence to inspire their approach, helping them recognize the unique needs of each situation. This service becomes more than an external action—it is an energetic commitment to uplift and support. By setting a foundation of intentional service, practitioners cultivate compassion, humility, and a willingness to allow their inner light to serve the greater good.

One important practice is "Energetic Clearing for Social Spaces," which involves applying Arcturian energy techniques to cleanse and elevate the energy of environments where community work takes place. Practitioners visualize the space filled with light, dissolving any discordant energies that may have accumulated. They see this light moving through walls, floors, and ceilings, bringing a sense of clarity and peace to the area. This cleansing can be done in spaces such as community centers, offices, or outdoor areas, creating an environment that feels welcoming and safe. Through this practice, practitioners establish a space that supports healing, open communication, and harmony, reinforcing the collective work that unfolds within it.

Another foundational technique introduced is "Community Connection Meditation," where practitioners tune into the collective energy of a specific group or community, focusing on understanding and compassion. In meditation, they imagine themselves connecting to the essence of the community, feeling its unique qualities, strengths, and challenges. This practice allows practitioners to align with the group's energy, building empathy and sensitivity that enhances their effectiveness in social projects. By connecting to the community in this way, they attune their actions with the authentic needs of the people they serve, promoting unity and respect.

Practitioners also engage in "Arcturian Empowerment Circles," where they gather with others who share similar intentions to create a collective field of energy focused on social healing. Participants hold hands or sit in a circle, visualizing the Arcturian light flowing through each person and merging at the center. Together, they set a shared intention for a specific project or cause, feeling this intention amplified as it circulates within the group. Empowerment circles allow practitioners to witness the increased strength of collective energy, demonstrating how working together with focused intent magnifies the potential for positive change.

To further develop their social work, practitioners are introduced to "Spiritual Mentorship and Guidance," a practice where they offer insights and support to individuals or groups within the community who seek growth and healing. Practitioners allow the Arcturian presence to guide their words and actions, fostering a space of trust where others feel safe to explore their spiritual potential. In this role, they do not position themselves as leaders but as facilitators, gently encouraging others to connect with their own inner strength. Through spiritual mentorship, practitioners embody humility, recognizing that true service is not about personal recognition but about uplifting and empowering others.

Another transformative practice in this phase is "Healing Projects Visualization," where practitioners visualize their social projects as fields of light, infused with Arcturian energy and aligned with the highest intentions. In meditation, they see each project—whether it involves wellness, education, or environmental care—as a radiant space filled with support and inspiration. Practitioners allow this visualization to expand, imagining the ripple effect of their efforts reaching those in need, fostering well-being and growth. Through this practice, they reinforce their dedication to social service, recognizing that even subtle energetic contributions can bring profound change.

In each of these practices, practitioners experience the joy of aligning their spiritual path with tangible social impact. They witness firsthand the transformative potential of Arcturian energy when applied to collective causes, observing how each act of service becomes a contribution to a wider field of healing and growth.

As practitioners deepen their work in social projects, they learn to integrate spiritual principles in ways that bring transformative, lasting impact to communities and the environment. This phase focuses on advanced techniques for applying Arcturian energy in social and ecological initiatives, emphasizing the power of aligned, conscious actions to foster collective healing. Practitioners come to see social projects not as separate from their spiritual path, but as profound expressions of it, where their highest intentions serve the greater good.

A significant practice here is "Energy-Infused Planning," where practitioners begin any project by visualizing it infused with Arcturian light. Before initiating the practical steps of a social initiative—whether it involves wellness, education, or environmental care—practitioners sit in meditation and envision the project's energy blueprint. They see the Arcturian energy moving through each stage, harmonizing efforts and aligning resources with the highest intention. Through this planning, they sense the pathways that hold the most potential for growth and transformation. This process allows practitioners to move forward with a clear, grounded vision, creating an energetic foundation that supports the project's success.

Another core technique is "Collective Energy Anchoring," where practitioners anchor Arcturian light into the spaces and communities affected by their work. During meditation, they imagine a pillar of Arcturian energy descending from above, grounding it deeply into the physical space of the project—whether a community center, a school, or a natural environment. This pillar of light serves as a stabilizing force, promoting a peaceful, nurturing atmosphere that supports everyone who interacts with it. By anchoring this energy, practitioners create a lasting impact, imbuing the space with a sense of harmony and protection that endures beyond their direct involvement.

Practitioners are introduced to "Ecological Healing Circles," designed specifically for environmental projects. In this practice, they gather in groups—physically or remotely—and focus on a specific ecological need, such as reforestation, water purification, or wildlife protection. Together, they visualize Arcturian energy flowing into the Earth, restoring balance and vitality to the natural elements involved. Practitioners hold the intention that their energy serves as a support for the planet's inherent healing processes. This practice not only contributes energetically to environmental well-being but also deepens practitioners' connection with nature, fostering a sense of responsibility and respect for all living systems.

A powerful practice in this phase is "Guided Group Visualization for Social Harmony," where practitioners lead others in visualizing a harmonious, compassionate society. In this guided session, participants imagine communities where understanding, cooperation, and mutual support are the norm. As they visualize this harmonious society, they focus on specific qualities, such as empathy, inclusiveness, and respect, allowing the energy of these qualities to expand outward. By guiding others in this visualization, practitioners activate a collective intention for social harmony, planting seeds of positive change that resonate within each participant and extend into their actions.

Another practice that supports advanced social projects is "Project Reflection and Gratitude," where practitioners regularly revisit the progress of their work, focusing on the positive impacts and lessons learned. In quiet reflection, they give gratitude for the connections formed, the support received, and the growth experienced through the project. This practice allows practitioners to remain humble and receptive, recognizing that each project is a journey of mutual exchange, where they also receive insight and inspiration. Practitioners feel the Arcturian guidance present in these reflections, reminding them of the interconnectedness of their efforts with the broader tapestry of healing and support.

Practitioners also learn "Empowering Community Leadership," a practice designed to foster leadership in others. Here, the practitioner's role is to empower individuals within the community to take initiative, offering encouragement and support rather than directing. Practitioners focus on identifying potential leaders, offering them tools and confidence to carry forward the project's goals. Guided by Arcturian energy, practitioners find ways to pass on knowledge and inspire others to become active participants. This approach ensures that the project can continue sustainably, with the community itself taking ownership and pride in the work being done.

As practitioners deepen their work in social and environmental projects, they witness the cumulative effect of their efforts. Each act of service—infused with Arcturian energy, mindful intention, and compassion—contributes to a wider field of positive change. Through each initiative, they experience firsthand the profound potential of spiritual practice when combined with purposeful action, realizing that the energies cultivated on their spiritual path resonate outward, fostering growth, healing, and unity. In this phase, practitioners become more than participants; they become stewards of collective well-being, recognizing that the path of spiritual evolution is one that embraces, supports, and uplifts all aspects of life.

Chapter 26
Collective Elevation

In exploring collective elevation, practitioners begin to focus on raising the vibrational field of groups and spaces, cultivating a powerful energy that supports both individual and shared spiritual growth. Arcturian guidance here deepens the understanding of how collective intentions amplify energy, creating harmonious environments that foster mutual support and transformation. Practitioners learn techniques for aligning the energy of groups to create an atmosphere filled with balance and resonance, benefiting all who enter these spaces.

Central to this journey is the "Circle of Elevation" practice, in which practitioners gather in a circle—either physically or through intention in meditation—envisioning a beam of Arcturian light anchoring in the center. Each participant connects with this central light, feeling it unify the circle with a shared purpose of elevation. Through deep breathing and focused visualization, practitioners sense the individual energies merging into a singular field, amplifying the resonance of the group. This Circle of Elevation becomes a space for transformation, as the collective field created acts as a catalyst for spiritual insights, healing, and peace.

Another foundational technique is "Space Harmonization," aimed at creating environments where elevated energy can be sustained. Practitioners engage in visualization and energy-infusing exercises, seeing the Arcturian light flow through the space and aligning its energetic patterns. They walk through the environment, mindful of each area, visualizing harmony and serenity filling every corner. The technique not only enhances the overall energy but also brings a sense of calm and clarity to all who enter, making it an ideal practice for spaces meant for meditation, group work, or even daily activities. Through Space Harmonization, practitioners learn to embed this elevated frequency into everyday spaces, creating pockets of peace and resonance.

"Resonance Alignment" is another transformative practice that focuses on harmonizing the frequencies of each participant within the group. Practitioners visualize Arcturian light flowing into their energy fields, aligning and balancing each person's vibration to foster harmony. As they engage in this alignment, they allow any discordant energies to gently release, feeling their field synchronize with others in the group. Through this shared alignment, they experience a deep connection with each other, sensing the unique contributions each person brings to the collective frequency. Resonance Alignment fosters an experience of unity, showing that, despite individual energies, a cohesive and uplifting atmosphere is possible.

A particularly profound practice introduced in this phase is the "Heart Coherence Meditation." Here, practitioners focus on synchronizing their heart energies, seeing them as radiant centers of light pulsing in unison. They visualize their hearts expanding, allowing the Arcturian light to flow through them, connecting each heart to form an interconnected field of compassion, love, and understanding. This Heart Coherence Meditation brings a deep sense of oneness, as the collective energy is elevated by the frequency of unconditional love. It demonstrates that when hearts resonate together, an elevated, nurturing energy becomes accessible to all, amplifying collective intention.

Another technique for raising group energy is "Group Intentions for Peace," a practice in which practitioners collectively focus on sending intentions of peace and harmony to a specific group, space, or situation. They gather together, either in person or in thought, to form a shared visualization of peace, each person contributing their unique energy to the vision. The group feels the Arcturian presence guiding their collective intention, seeing this energy ripple outward to touch the intended area or people. Group Intentions for Peace show how collective focus can extend beyond the immediate environment, demonstrating the broader impact of shared, high-vibrational intentions on a global scale.

Practitioners also begin the "Elevation Anchor" practice, a technique where they focus on anchoring the elevated collective energy to a specific intention, such as personal growth, healing, or support for the world. Through visualization and Arcturian light guidance, practitioners see this anchored intention as a stable source of elevated energy. They are encouraged to revisit this anchor regularly, reinforcing the collective energy tied to this purpose. The Elevation Anchor allows practitioners to carry forward the benefits of collective work, ensuring that the high-vibrational field created in each gathering can be sustained and drawn upon in future moments.

Through these practices, practitioners experience the potency of aligned group energy and the expanded impact of working toward a shared, elevated state. They come to understand that when individuals unite with common intention, a powerful field of transformation and harmony emerges. This approach emphasizes the beauty of collective evolution, showing that spiritual growth is not only personal but deeply interconnected with others. Practitioners come to appreciate that every elevated gathering adds to a wider, resonant field of peace and compassion that has the potential to uplift not just the participants, but the collective consciousness as a whole.

Deepening the journey into collective elevation, practitioners refine and expand their skills to amplify and stabilize elevated frequencies in large groups and environments. Here, Arcturian techniques focus on anchoring spiritual energies with such potency that they reverberate far beyond the immediate setting, creating lasting impacts that support ongoing collective harmony. This stage delves into advanced practices that allow practitioners to become conduits of Arcturian light, fostering peace, balance, and elevated awareness in spaces and gatherings of various scales.

One of the core practices introduced is the "Pillars of Light Technique." Practitioners envision powerful columns of Arcturian energy descending into the space from above, forming a network of luminous pillars throughout the environment. Each pillar acts as a stabilizing force, harmonizing and balancing the frequencies within the area. Practitioners guide the energy of these pillars to anchor into the Earth, allowing the elevated vibrations to be absorbed and retained within the physical space. As they move through the environment, they sense how these pillars create a supportive energetic grid, generating a protective, calm, and elevated atmosphere that endures well beyond their physical presence.

In this phase, practitioners also engage in the "Vibrational Tuning Practice," where they synchronize the energy of large groups, harmonizing the unique frequencies of each participant to align with the collective vibration. This practice involves gathering the group in focused meditation, where practitioners guide the Arcturian light to envelop everyone, gently adjusting any energetic disparities. They envision the group's individual energies blending into a cohesive, radiant field that resonates with peace and elevated awareness. Through this unified frequency, participants experience a profound connection and openness, fostering an environment where personal and collective insights emerge effortlessly.

A more advanced technique introduced here is "Chakra Harmonization for Collective Fields." In this practice, practitioners visualize a vast, energetic chakra system encompassing the entire group, symbolizing the collective energy centers. As they attune each chakra, from root to crown, they see Arcturian energy infusing each center, aligning and balancing it. This harmonization serves to unify the group's emotional, mental, and spiritual states, allowing participants to experience elevated insights and deeper interconnectedness. Chakra Harmonization for Collective Fields becomes a powerful tool for aligning intentions, deepening the shared experience, and maintaining the energetic integrity of large gatherings.

The "Resonant Sound Practice" further enhances the collective vibration by using sound as a conduit for Arcturian energy. Practitioners introduce toning, chanting, or instrumental sounds, allowing each resonance to carry the frequency of light throughout the environment. The Arcturian energy merges with the sound waves, amplifying the vibration in ways that align and harmonize everyone present. As the sounds reverberate, practitioners visualize them filling the entire space with a transformative frequency, which imbues the group with peace, clarity, and spiritual openness. Resonant Sound Practice illustrates the power of sound in cultivating collective elevation, creating an immersive experience that touches each participant deeply.

Another profound practice introduced is "Heart Resonance Expansion," where practitioners focus on expanding the collective heart energy of the group. In this exercise, they envision Arcturian light flowing through their heart centers and connecting with those around them, creating an unbroken field of love and compassion. They sense how each individual's heart energy merges with the collective field, forming a vast and encompassing vibration that pulses with unconditional love. This resonance fosters a nurturing environment where participants feel safe, open, and supported, allowing deeper bonds and shared intentions to form organically.

Practitioners also explore "Environmental Anchoring," a practice that focuses on anchoring elevated vibrations within specific physical locations, such as community spaces, natural sites, or frequently visited areas. By visualizing Arcturian light deeply embedding into the foundations of these spaces, practitioners intend that the elevated energy remains present, creating a field that influences all who enter. Environmental Anchoring becomes a way for practitioners to extend the benefits of their gatherings, establishing lasting sanctuaries of peace, compassion, and harmony that radiate outward into the broader community.

This advanced phase of collective elevation reveals to practitioners the profound influence of unified spiritual intentions. As they integrate these practices, they recognize that the elevated energy fields they create contribute to a greater network of light that resonates beyond any one gathering or space. Through this deepening process, practitioners come to understand that each elevated group becomes part of a vast, interconnected field of consciousness, contributing to the wider spiritual evolution of humanity. Practitioners embrace their role as facilitators of collective harmony, knowing that every elevated interaction creates ripples of transformation that resonate far and wide.

Chapter 27
Planetary Consciousness

In the journey towards planetary consciousness, practitioners begin to explore the profound connection between individual spirituality and the collective evolution of Earth. Here, the Arcturian guidance emphasizes the importance of unity with all beings, fostering a consciousness that transcends personal growth and expands into a compassionate awareness of the planet as a living entity. Through these practices, practitioners align their spiritual paths with a universal purpose, engaging in exercises that not only enhance personal consciousness but contribute to a global field of healing and harmony.

One central practice is the "Earth Connection Meditation," where practitioners establish a grounding connection with the planet's energy. Visualizing roots extending from their feet deep into the Earth, they feel the steady, nurturing pulse of the planet's core. Guided by Arcturian light, they attune to Earth's rhythms and feel themselves blending with its energy, experiencing a sense of oneness with the planet. This meditation deepens awareness of the Earth's needs and allows practitioners to sense shifts in planetary energy, cultivating a protective and symbiotic relationship with the natural world.

"Planetary Breath Alignment" is introduced as a technique to synchronize with the Earth's pulse. Practitioners breathe deeply, visualizing the Earth's breath rising and falling with their own, creating a rhythm that aligns their energy with the planet's frequency. Each inhale draws in Arcturian energy from the universe, which practitioners direct into the Earth with each exhale, intending healing, peace, and balance. Planetary Breath Alignment fosters a deep resonance with Earth's energetic layers, creating a mutually beneficial flow of energy that supports both personal well-being and planetary harmony.

The "Network of Light" visualization practice focuses on expanding one's consciousness to encompass the planet as a whole. In meditation, practitioners envision a vast web of Arcturian light encircling the Earth, connecting energy centers across continents, oceans, and landscapes. They imagine this network linking all beings—humans, animals, plants, and even the elements—within a luminous field that pulses with unity and compassion. Through this practice, practitioners contribute to a collective consciousness of light, strengthening a global field that nurtures planetary healing and conscious evolution.

"Elemental Connection" is another essential practice in this phase, where practitioners tune into Earth's elemental forces—earth, water, fire, and air. In meditation, they visualize each element as a distinct energy, with the Arcturian light harmonizing and balancing these forces within themselves and the surrounding environment. Practitioners focus on each element's qualities, such as stability from earth, flow from water, warmth from fire, and clarity from air, experiencing how these energies shape the planet's natural cycles. This practice fosters an understanding of how aligning with Earth's elements enhances personal and collective harmony, leading to a deeper appreciation of nature's interconnected wisdom.

Practitioners then explore "Planetary Gratitude Offering," a ritual to express gratitude towards Earth. They gather natural items, like stones, leaves, or seeds, and imbue them with intentions of love, respect, and protection. Through visualization, they infuse each item with Arcturian light and place them at a designated spot in nature, offering their blessings back to the planet. This ritual creates a sacred exchange, where practitioners honor the Earth for its abundance and support. The act of giving back, however simple, opens channels for deeper planetary connection and mutual sustenance, reinforcing a sense of responsibility towards Earth's well-being.

"Arcturian Vision for Earth" becomes an advanced meditative journey, where practitioners receive insights into the Arcturian vision of Earth's potential. Guided by the Arcturian light, they journey in meditation to see Earth from an elevated perspective, sensing its energetic pathways, natural structures, and hidden potential. Practitioners perceive visions of a harmonious world, where ecosystems flourish, and humanity exists in balance with nature. Through this vision, they gain a renewed sense of purpose and understand how their personal actions contribute to this planetary transformation. The Arcturian Vision for Earth inspires practitioners to align their intentions with this greater vision, fostering unity and harmony with all life.

This journey into planetary consciousness marks a profound shift in practitioners' awareness, encouraging them to transcend personal goals and embrace a collective, Earth-centered consciousness. Through these practices, practitioners recognize their role within a vast network of beings, each contributing to a global elevation. With the Arcturian guidance, they become stewards of planetary harmony, dedicated to fostering a balanced, peaceful world that reflects the unity and compassion cultivated within.

As practitioners deepen their engagement with planetary consciousness, they explore advanced Arcturian techniques designed to harmonize their energy with Earth's evolving vibration. This part delves into methods for channeling healing frequencies to the planet, refining awareness of Earth's energetic shifts, and nurturing a sustained sense of global unity. Practitioners expand their role as co-creators in planetary evolution, aligning their intentions with the rhythms of nature and enhancing the Earth's journey toward collective enlightenment.

One of the central practices here is the "Planetary Healing Pulse." Practitioners visualize a stream of Arcturian light descending through them, directed into the Earth as a rhythmic pulse. With each breath, they send this pulse deep into the planet's core, intending it to flow through Earth's energy grids. As the light spreads across these pathways, it balances and revitalizes areas experiencing energetic depletion or imbalance. Practitioners sense how the healing pulse creates subtle yet transformative vibrations, supporting the Earth's own restorative processes and weaving light into the physical and energetic fabric of the planet.

The "Global Heart Connection" exercise serves to align practitioners' heart energies with Earth's heartbeat. Guided by Arcturian energy, practitioners place their hands over their heart and visualize their heartbeat merging with the rhythm of the planet. As the connection strengthens, they feel a profound sense of unity with all life. Practitioners imagine this shared heartbeat resonating outward, linking them with the hearts of all beings and forming a planetary field of compassion. This field becomes a source of stability, especially in times of global upheaval, as practitioners contribute their love and empathy to strengthen Earth's collective resilience.

An advanced practice called "Ley Line Activation" is introduced, where practitioners focus on the Earth's natural energy lines, or ley lines, which carry powerful currents across the planet. Guided by Arcturian insight, practitioners attune to these lines in meditation, visualizing streams of light flowing along them, connecting sacred sites and energetic hotspots around the world. They mentally trace these paths, amplifying the flow with Arcturian energy to clear any blockages and ensure a harmonious current. Through this practice, practitioners help maintain a balanced and vibrant energy system that sustains Earth's vitality and enhances the well-being of all its inhabitants.

"Gaian Resonance Alignment" draws practitioners' awareness to Earth's own frequency, often known as the Schumann resonance. Guided by the Arcturians, practitioners align their meditation to match this frequency, creating a state of resonance with the planet's vibration. As they synchronize, they experience a deep sense of stability and interconnectedness, feeling how their energy merges seamlessly with Earth's. This alignment not only harmonizes practitioners with natural rhythms but also enhances their sensitivity to shifts in Earth's energy. Practitioners learn to recognize these fluctuations, becoming attuned to moments when Earth may need additional energetic support.

In the "Sacred Elemental Circles" practice, practitioners deepen their relationship with the elements of Earth, Water, Fire, and Air. They gather small representations of each element, such as stones, water, a candle, and a feather, and place them in a circle. Calling upon the Arcturian energy, they channel light into each item, honoring it as a living part of Earth's consciousness. They then visualize the elements blending and forming a radiant sphere that pulses with balanced, harmonious energy. This sphere becomes a concentrated source of elemental harmony that practitioners can direct toward areas of environmental imbalance or offer as a gift of alignment to the planet.

"Universal Field Projection" expands practitioners' awareness beyond Earth to the cosmic forces that influence planetary evolution. In meditation, they visualize Earth enveloped within a cosmic field of Arcturian light, sensing how this field connects to the greater universe. Practitioners project an intention of harmony, visualizing a delicate web of light linking Earth to other celestial bodies, symbolizing Earth's role within the vast network of the cosmos. This projection reinforces the sense of planetary consciousness as a part of a universal whole, where Earth's energy shifts are in harmony with the cosmic evolution unfolding around it.

The "Guardianship Intention" practice deepens practitioners' commitment to Earth's protection and elevation. In this practice, they create a personal affirmation or intention of guardianship over the planet, acknowledging their role in sustaining harmony and peace. Guided by the Arcturian light, they visualize their commitment radiating outward, anchoring into the Earth as a promise of care and respect. Practitioners sense this affirmation merging with the collective field of others who hold similar intentions, creating a global web of guardianship dedicated to Earth's well-being. This practice empowers practitioners with a sense of shared purpose, reinforcing their connection to the planet and to all who walk a similar path of stewardship.Through these advanced practices, practitioners anchor a continuous consciousness of planetary unity and harmony. They cultivate an intuitive bond with the Earth, where the boundaries between personal and planetary well-being dissolve, allowing them to act as channels of transformative energy for the planet. Each practice serves as a reminder of their connection to the Arcturian vision, where personal evolution and planetary consciousness blend into a shared path, guiding Earth and its inhabitants towards an elevated, harmonious state of being.

Chapter 28
Collective Transcendence

As the journey draws near its zenith, the Arcturian teachings guide practitioners into the realm of collective transcendence, where personal growth melds seamlessly with humanity's evolution. Practitioners are invited to embody and embrace the vision of a unified collective, transcending individual limitations and stepping into a role that contributes to the consciousness of all beings. Here, the Arcturians illuminate a path that calls for both profound inner transformation and outward alignment, creating a bridge between the self and the vast network of life that pulses across the universe.

One of the foundational practices is the "Unity Consciousness Meditation," where practitioners gather their awareness inward, envisioning their consciousness expanding beyond the self, encompassing all humanity, and stretching across the web of life. Guided by the Arcturian light, they sense the interconnectedness of each individual, feeling how personal choices, intentions, and energies contribute to the whole. Practitioners enter a meditative state in which boundaries between individual selves dissolve, opening them to the collective experience of humankind, sensing joy, sorrow, growth, and hope as shared aspects of one unified soul.

Another essential practice, the "Arcturian Heart Activation," strengthens practitioners' capacity to channel love and compassion to all beings. This exercise focuses on the heart center, visualizing it as a radiant sphere of Arcturian light. Through breathwork, practitioners allow this light to expand, enveloping others, transcending distances, and reaching individuals, communities, and nations. As the heart's energy extends outward, practitioners experience an intense sense of empathy and solidarity, feeling the universal bond that links every being. Through this practice, the heart's capacity to hold the collective deepens, fortifying practitioners as vessels of compassion.

The "Vision of the New Earth" practice invites practitioners to explore the Arcturian vision for an evolved Earth. In a guided visualization, they enter a meditative space where they see the Earth transformed—its energy luminous, vibrant, and free from discord. They see communities thriving in harmony, humanity existing in peaceful symbiosis with nature, and all beings honored as sacred facets of a unified whole. Practitioners feel their intentions aligning with this vision, becoming architects of this emerging reality. This practice instills a deep-seated sense of purpose, encouraging them to embody qualities that resonate with the vision of an evolved world.

"Transcendent Breathwork" brings practitioners into a state of collective resonance with the universal life force. Using a rhythmic, intentional breathing technique, they imagine each inhale as drawing energy from the universe, infusing it with their intentions for collective elevation, and exhaling this intention outward, amplifying it through the energy field that surrounds them. With each breath, they send waves of harmonious intent into the collective consciousness, contributing their energy to a shared, uplifting pulse. This practice awakens a heightened awareness of each individual's ability to impact the whole, bridging personal intention with global transformation.

The "Anchoring Peace Technique" is introduced as a method to contribute to global tranquility during times of tension or discord. Practitioners ground themselves in Arcturian light, stabilizing their energy, and visualize the Earth bathed in a peaceful, soothing light. Guided by the Arcturian presence, they direct calming energy to areas of need, focusing on regions affected by conflict or distress. This technique instills a sense of responsibility and agency, allowing practitioners to consciously anchor frequencies of peace within the collective energy field, reinforcing a more balanced global atmosphere.

Another vital exercise, the "Web of Intentions," uses visualization to cultivate unity among practitioners with shared intentions for planetary well-being. In meditation, practitioners envision a web of golden threads stretching across the globe, connecting them to others who hold similar aspirations for healing, growth, and harmony. Each practitioner contributes their light, sensing how these threads strengthen, creating a resilient network dedicated to positive change. This web becomes a living manifestation of collective transcendence, a channel through which transformative intentions flow, amplified by the union of like-hearted individuals.

The "Arcturian Pillar of Transcendence" practice allows practitioners to act as conduits of elevated energy for the world. Visualizing themselves as a pillar of Arcturian light, they anchor this transcendent energy from the cosmos to Earth, bridging higher frequencies into the collective field. This practice calls for a profound commitment, inviting practitioners to become stabilizing anchors for the flow of Arcturian energy. As they embody this light, they reinforce Earth's ascension, contributing their presence to the subtle shifts that guide humanity toward higher consciousness.

Collective transcendence represents the harmonious blending of individual evolution and shared purpose, calling forth qualities that serve both personal growth and planetary ascension. Through these practices, practitioners recognize their lives as threads in the fabric of a collective awakening. They perceive the Arcturian guidance not merely as a personal journey but as a shared commitment to elevate the consciousness of all beings, stepping into their roles as catalysts in a transformative vision that resonates through the cosmos.

In this culminating phase of the journey, the Arcturian teachings converge into a unified vision, expanding individual transformation into a continuous stream of collective light. Practitioners, having woven each practice into their lives, now explore the power of transcendence as an eternal and universal current. This state of being goes beyond simple spiritual evolution; it is the synthesis of every inner growth, each healing intention, and all awakened consciousness shared with humanity and all realms of existence.

The "Sacred Continuum Meditation" serves as a foundational practice in achieving this timeless state of collective transcendence. As practitioners enter a meditative state, they visualize their essence merging into a boundless stream of energy that flows endlessly through all beings and realms, guided by the Arcturian light. In this timeless flow, practitioners feel themselves not as isolated entities but as currents within an ocean of transcendence. This practice opens their awareness to the perpetual unity that bonds every soul, fostering an unshakable peace and serenity as they witness the shared journey of all life.

One powerful method for reinforcing this bond is the "Legacy of Light Visualization," a practice that channels practitioners' intentions and achievements into the future. Guided by Arcturian energy, they envision their personal growth and healing efforts as seeds planted within the collective consciousness. These seeds take form as luminous particles, moving beyond the present and spreading into future generations. Each action, each moment of compassion, becomes an eternal gift to humanity's collective heart. In this visualization, practitioners understand that their own awakening fuels a lasting continuum of light, embodying a transcendent legacy.

The "Vortex of Transcendence" exercise builds upon previous practices, guiding practitioners into the creation of an energetic vortex that absorbs and radiates Arcturian frequencies. This vortex, visualized as a spiraling light, acts as a bridge between Earthly existence and higher realms. In meditation, practitioners envision this vortex enveloping not just themselves, but communities, ecosystems, and even global spheres of influence. As they expand this energy field, they feel a deepened capacity to bridge collective consciousness with transcendent realms, facilitating the infusion of wisdom, harmony, and balance into the Earth's energetic layers.

As practitioners deepen this path, the "Resonance of All Beings" meditation extends their awareness into the multidimensional nature of the universe. Guided by Arcturian presence, they explore the subtle vibrations that connect all forms of life across different planes. This meditation reveals the symphony of existence, where each being resonates as a note within a cosmic composition. Practitioners find harmony within this vast resonance, experiencing how their individual vibration aligns with the collective symphony, bringing harmony to both their own frequency and the planetary energy field.

The "Circle of Guardianship" ritual fosters a network of practitioners, transcending time and space as they create an etheric circle dedicated to collective transcendence. They envision themselves standing together in a circle, joined by other souls across dimensions, holding intentions of healing, peace, and elevation for all beings. This circle becomes a portal through which Arcturian energy flows continuously, a guardian force that sustains the vibrational integrity of humanity and Earth. Through this exercise, practitioners deepen their role as protectors of transcendent energy, fortifying their commitment to sustaining the collective journey.

In a further step, the "Luminous Echoes" practice allows practitioners to anchor their intentions within the universe's energetic fabric. During this exercise, they visualize each of their practices, thoughts, and actions creating echoes that expand infinitely, touching all beings and realms. Guided by the Arcturians, they feel these echoes resounding within the universal memory, a testament to humanity's ascent toward higher consciousness. This technique affirms the enduring impact of each practitioner's path, instilling an awareness of their purpose within the greater cosmic evolution.

The "Transcendent Channeling of Light" solidifies practitioners' ability to be continuous conduits for Arcturian energy. In this exercise, they visualize themselves as vessels through which the Arcturian light flows without obstruction, pouring continuously from cosmic realms into Earth's field. Practitioners learn to maintain this channel, not as a temporary practice but as an ongoing flow that aligns with daily life. They become embodiments of Arcturian wisdom, radiating healing energy and higher awareness with each interaction, action, and thought, solidifying their roles as living pillars of transcendence.

With these practices, practitioners embrace their journey as both personal and collective, extending beyond the limitations of the present moment. The teachings transform into a living current, moving through each practitioner into the world, blending the temporal and the eternal in the service of humanity's ascension. The Arcturians impart that true transcendence is not an ending but a continual state of openness and unity, a perpetual movement toward higher states of harmony and understanding. Practitioners become not only receivers of light but bearers, infusing their lives and the lives they touch with the sacred essence of collective transcendence. Through this embodiment, they contribute to the gradual awakening of a world bound by love, healed through unity, and elevated by an ever-expanding consciousness that bridges Earth with the cosmos.

Epilogue

At the end of this reading, there is something beyond words—a call to internalize the experience you have lived here and to let it become a part of who you are. This book, more than a collection of teachings, has become a bridge, a link that has connected you to the infinite, awakening in you the understanding that everything is connected. Now, as you close these pages, carry with you not only the ideas, but the energy and wisdom that flowed through each paragraph, each practice, resonating within every cell of your being.

The journey does not end here. On the contrary, it now expands into your life, allowing the teachings of the Arcturians and the discoveries you made to become a living practice, a constant reminder of your connection with the universe. Every insight, every moment of peace you experienced through this reading are seeds that, when nurtured, will blossom, guiding you along new paths with greater clarity, compassion, and purpose.

What you take from this book is more than a series of spiritual practices; it is a constant reminder that the power of transformation lies within you. You are a vibrant being, full of potential, and this reading was only the beginning of a process of self-discovery and expansion that will continue to guide you, unfolding deeper layers of your being. Each energy alignment practice, each moment of meditation and connection with the Arcturians is a step toward a higher consciousness, an opening to the flow of energy and wisdom that surrounds you.

The wisdom gained here does not belong to the past; it is a beacon that lights your path, allowing you to walk with the certainty that, as you awaken to your essence, you impact not only your life, but the world around you. The energy you harmonized within yourself reverberates through the world, connecting you to the greater purpose of peace and harmony that the Arcturians continually promote. And as you integrate these truths, you realize that spiritual growth is an eternal gift, an ascending spiral that continues to expand your perception and your capacity to love.

Now, with the flame of understanding ignited within, the path ahead is clear, even if unknown. This reading was a preparation, a purification that opened your heart and mind to realms of true awareness. From this point on, you are called to transform your own life into a reflection of this wisdom, applying the teachings and nurturing the peace, light, and love that have awakened within you. Be, therefore, a point of light in the world, an anchor of peace and healing, radiating the qualities that now resonate in your essence.

Connected to the universe, to the Arcturians, and to wisdom that transcends the visible, continue on your journey knowing that awakening is a continuous state, a constant invitation to the soul's refinement. With each step forward, remember that this transformation is only the beginning of something much greater, a constant reminder that you are part of a vast, loving whole. May your journey be guided by the light and wisdom gained here, and may you, with courage and gratitude, continue to explore the dimensions now opening before you.

www.ingramcontent.com/pod-product-compliance
Lightning Source LLC
LaVergne TN
LVHW040146080526
838202LV00042B/3045